Winning Words from Football Greats

Larry Bielat

COACHES CHOICE™

ISBN: 1-58518-917-0
Library of Congress Control Number: 2004113792
Cover design: Jeanne Hamilton
Book layout: Jeanne Hamilton

Coaches Choice
P.O. Box 1828
Monterey, CA 93942
www.coacheschoice.com

Dedication

To Bruno Marana and Bill Chmelko, my high school football coaches at Center Line Michigan who started my love for the game, and to my Panther teammates who won two Michican State Championships. Also to my Uncle Vince, who never missed a game, and his son Paul, for their encouragement.

Acknowledgments

The author gratefully acknowledges the sports information directors who provided photos and background information, and Paula Montayne, Mark Schubert, and Jason Fields for their expert assistance.

Special thanks go to Pamela Schubert, for her help with everything from research to typing.

Pamela Schubert

The Game of Football

A College President in 1960 to the American Football Coaches Association

There is much more to football than passing, running, and kicking. There is also discipline, a competitive spirit, and courage. By teaching men of tomorrow these qualities, you, the football coaches, are helping your country more than maybe you realize. The same qualities you give meaning to on the playing field are the ones your players will carry with them into the next century. And the qualities they, in turn, will pass on to their children in years ahead—discipline, competitive spirit, courage. With them our country can survive forever. Without them, tomorrow is in doubt.

Contents

Football Greats

Introduction

Football is an American game uniquely different from any other sport in the world. It's a war game of attack and defend. A man's game that calls for physical fitness and mental quickness, but above all, courage. It's a game that grips communities, fills stadiums, and rivets millions to TV sets during the football season.

Intensely loyal fans go into a fury when Canton McKinley High School plays Massillon in Ohio, or when Florida takes on Florida State, or the Green Bay Packers invade Soldier Field in Chicago. Nothing in sport compares.

In this book I have tried to gather the feelings of the game, through the words of great coaches, players, and writers. Many winners are absent. They got the job done without being often quoted. Included also are comments by presidents, generals, and others often used around football locker rooms.

In some cases I had to edit a quote for clarity. Many of the items came second- or third-hand, and so may not be written exactly as first stated. Every effort was made to capture the intent.

I have had direct contact with some of the men on the following pages. Duffy Daugherty was my coach at Michigan State and I was recruited by one of his assistants, Bob Devaney. Eddie Robinson, Jake Gaither, Bear Bryant, and Bud Wilkinson visited Duffy in East Lansing and often spoke at his clinics.

In my 20 years at State as an assistant coach and broadcaster, I attended many meetings with Woody, Bo, Hayden Fry, Joe Paterno, and Leo Holtz. I always took notes. George Perles and I were teammates and friends and later coached high school, college, and pro football together. I have tried to capture the heart and soul of the game from all these men. I hope you enjoy my effort.

What Is Football?

Tonto Coleman
The SEC's Third Commissioner

It's a wild and wonderful combination of intelligence, dumbness, speed, agility, and a large helping of violence.

Outsiders may be thrilled by the spectacle of football, but non-combatants will never fully know what the game really means to those who risk their bones to play it. Only a participant can understand its true nature. Only a man who has left a little of himself on the field can love football with almost a religious passion.

Football is not a game where losing is tolerated. It is a game of oaths and slogans and battle cries. The emphasis is always on winning, regardless of the naïve poems about "playing the game." The coach who strings victories together as a diamond necklace is coddled like an Oriental despot and then after a losing season hung in effigy. It is the way the code operates. Everyone understands that stragglers are shot.

What is football?

It's a shocking upset every now and then. It is Chicken Little Tech rising in a mighty wrath and blowing Moose Jaw U out of the Top Ten. It is some skinny sophomore who wants to play making a second stringer of last year's All-American who thought he had it made.

What is football?

It's a 10-year professional, just retired, showing a sportswriter the place where his right knee bones used to be. It is foul weather on the last weekend and the season ticket holders huddled together, insanely risking their health to see that sophomore halfback break the school rushing record. And football is a big lug of a left tackle choking as he sings the alma mater on graduation day with tears leaking down his beefy, battered cheeks, already worrying about how he'll feel next fall when he has to wear wing-tips instead of cleats.

Football as War

From General George Patton's "Wisdom of War" 1933

Wars may be fought with weapons, but they are won with men. It is the spirit of the men who follow and of the man who leads that gains the victory.

Accept the challenge so that you may feel the exhilaration.

I don't want any communiqués saying you are holding your position. We're not holding anything. We'll let the enemy try to hold on. We are attacking day and night every minute.

In the Words of General Douglas MacArthur

There is no security on this earth.
There is only opportunity.

Upon the field of friendly strife are sown the seeds that on other fields, on other days, will bear the fruits of victory.

Note: All coaches' records are current as of the beginning of the 2004 season.

Bobby Bowden
Florida State

Active

Born: Birmingham, Alabama
College: Howard, 1953
Coached: Samford, West Virginia, Florida State
Years: 38
Record: 342-99-4
Accomplishments:
- 32 bowl games (22 consecutive)
- 18 New Year's Day games
- 18 seasons with 10 or more wins
- 2 national championships

A coach is like an auto mechanic who has all the parts of a car laid out on the floor. He knows if there's one piece missing, the darn thing just won't work.

If you just keep hustling good things start to happen. As soon as you stop hustling you ain't got a chance.

Don't leave any regrets on the field.

He doesn't know the meaning of the word fear. In fact, I just saw his grades, and he doesn't know the meaning of a whole lot of words.

—Bowden, on one of his linebackers

Don't go to your grave with a life unused.

Bowden, when asked if discipline was the key to winning: If it were, Army, Navy, and the Air Force would be playing for the National Championship every year.

God doesn't want your ability. He wants your availability.

❖

Bowden hires assistant coaches in this manner—character first, intelligence second, men with class third, and football knowledge fourth.

❖

I've coached in the 50s, 60s, 70s, 80s, 90s, and now in the 2000s. Coaching now ain't even close to what it was in the 1950s. Times have changed. If a coach doesn't change, he's fixin' to get fired.

❖

Just win, that shuts everybody up.

❖

Each week in practice, work on the few things you're sure will work and get 'em right.

❖

You win by adapting—you've got to anticipate change.

❖

You don't want sameness on your staff.
You have to have a mix of go-getters and quiet ones.

❖

You start with loyalty—you to your school, your school to you, you to your staff, your staff to you.

❖

You cannot build a winning program without help from the media.
Be fair. Be open. Be careful.

❖

Winning is only part of the game.

Terry Bradshaw
Pittsburgh Steelers (Quarterback)

Born: Shreveport, Louisiana
College: Southeast Louisiana, 1970
Played: Pittsburgh Steelers
Accomplishments:
- 4 Super Bowl championships
- 2-time Super Bowl MVP
- NFL Hall of Fame, 1989
- TV sports celebrity

There Are a Few Left
Grantland Rice

Who put the game above the score,
Who rate the battle as the test,
Who stand content amid the roar,
Where they have given out their best;
No matter what the prize at stake,
Who prove that they can give—and take.
Who have no fear of some defeat,
No vain regrets to haunt their night,
Because the race went to the fleet,
Because the stronger won the fight;
Who do their stuff—win, lose or draw,
and laugh at fate's inconstant law.

Sometimes you may be scared to death, but don't admit it, even to yourself.

The heck with statistics. Just win!

Mistakes take away your confidence, and when you lose confidence, everything bad has a compounding effect on you. When an athlete is truly focusing, he or she doesn't hear the negative. It has no effect. That's control.

❖

Never try to make friends with your head coach.

❖

Enthusiasm
Presbyterian of the South

Enthusiasm is reason gone mad to achieve a definite, rational objective.

Enthusiasm is inflamed by opposition, but never converted; it is the leaping lightning that blasts obstacles from its path.

Enthusiasm is the X-ray of the soul, that penetrates and reveals the invisible.

Enthusiasm is a contagion that laughs at quarantine and inoculates all who come in contact with it.

Enthusiasm is the vibrant thrill in your voice that sways the will of others into harmony with your own.

Enthusiasm is the "philosopher's stone" that transmutes dull tasks into delightful deeds.

Enthusiasm is a magnet that draws kindred souls with irresistible force and electrifies them with the magnetism of its own resolves.

Frank Broyles
Arkansas

Born: Decatur, Georgia
College: Georgia Tech, 1947
Coached: Missouri, Arkansas
Years: 20
Record: 144-58-5
Accomplishments:
- SEC Player of the Year, 1946
- 10 bowl games
- 1 national championship
- 3 of Broyles' assistants have won national campionships—Barry Switzer, John Majors, and Jimmy Johnson.
- 3 of Broyles' assistants have won Super Bowls—Johnson, Switzer, and Joe Gibbs.

The team that won't be beaten can't be beaten.

The stands are for spectators, not the playing field.

Luck follows speed.

You don't think about or remember the close games you won. It's the close ones you lost that you can't forget.

If our game, football, is to be a preparation for life, then it must be more than relaxing play. Caesar put it well when he said: "Cowards die many times; the valiant taste of death but once."

Courage is one of the things our game of football teaches. The way to drain the life out of it is to take it lightly. I hope my players learn that neither winning nor losing is as important as what they learn about themselves during heated competition.

Paul "Bear" Bryant
Alabama

Born: Moro Bottoms, Arkansas
College: Alabama, 1936
Coached: Maryland, Kentucky, Texas A&M, Alabama
Years: 38
Record: 323-85-17
Accomplishments:

- 13 SEC Titles
- 3-time National Coach of the Year
- 10-time SEC Coach of the Year
- 72-2 at home (Bryant-Denny Stadium)
- 23-3-2 as a player at Alabama
- 38-12-6 as an assistant coach
- Took Alabama to 24 bowl games
- Never lost a Homecoming Game at Alabama (25-0)
- 29 bowl games
- 6 national championships

If you were to ask me if football is a coach's game, I'd have to say it is—and always was.

The definition of an atheist in Alabama is someone who doesn't believe in Bear Bryant.

—Wally Butts, coach, University of Georgia

Get your winners into the game. You can't win with your best players standing next to you on the sidelines.

If you get ahead, play like you're behind.

Bryant, on the three types of individuals who play the game: First, there are those who are winners and know they are winners. Then, there are the losers who know they are losers. Then, there are those who hate to lose, who want to win every play, every game. They're the ones for me. They never quit. They're the soul of our game.

There has got to be a special place in heaven for coaches' wives.

Bear, when asked by a reporter if it was true he could walk on water: Well, I won't say I can or I can't. But if I do, I do it before most people get up in the morning.

When we have a good team, I know it's because we have boys that come from good mommas and papas.

About recruiting—remember, you can't make good chicken salad without good chicken.

How do you win?
You start by out-conditioning your opponents.

Motivating people—the ingredient that separates winners from losers.

I don't hire anybody not brighter than I am.
If they're not smarter than me, I don't need them.

Good coaches win every game they ought to and a few they shouldn't.

Football changes and so do people. The successful coach is the one who sets the trend, not the one who follows it.

When you win, there's glory enough for everybody.
When you lose, there's glory for none.

Bear Bryant's Three Rules for Coaching

1. Surround yourself with people who can't live without football.
2. Recognize winners. They come in all forms.
3. Have a plan for everything.

Most folks don't plan. That's why it is easy to beat most folks.

If anything goes bad, I did it. If anything goes semi-good, we did it. If anything goes real good, you did it. That's all it takes to get people to win football games.

Every time a player goes out there, at least 20 people have some amount of influence on him. His Momma has more influence than anyone.

It's really very hard for the students and alumni to rally 'round a math class.
                    –Bryant, explaining the role of athletics at the university

The first time you quit, it's hard.
The second time, it gets easier.
The third time, you don't even think about it.

In a crisis, don't hide behind anything or anybody.
Remember, they're going to find you anyway.

It's not the will to win that matters. Everyone has that.
It's the will to prepare to win that matters.

I can reach a kid who doesn't have any ability as long as he doesn't know it.

I don't care how much talent a team has. If the boys don't think tough, practice tough, and live tough, they won't play tough on Saturday.

Sacrifice—Work—Self-discipline.
I teach these things, and my boys don't forget them when they leave.

When you make a mistake, admit it. Learn from it and don't repeat it.

In life, you'll have your back up against the wall many times. Become accustomed to it.

The alumni are starting to grumble, and I'm the alum who is starting it.
                    —Bryant, to the press after a close loss at Alabama

I'd do things differently now than when I started. I failed some of them early boys, but it was all I knew at the time.

Maybe the good Lord is kinda testing us to see what we got in us.

The first thing a football coach needs when he's starting out is a wife who's willing to put up with a whole lot of neglect. The second thing is a five-year contract.

No coach has ever won a game by what he knows;
it's what his players know that counts.

You must learn how to hold a team together. You lift some men up, calm others down, until finally when they got one heartbeat, you've got yourself a team.

The price of victory is high, but so are the rewards.

You never know how a horse will pull until you hook him to a heavy load.

In order to have a winner, the team must have a feeling of unity; every player must put the team first, ahead of personal glory. Morale is the key to winning.

Take those little rascals, talk to them good, pat them on the back, let them think they are good, and they will go out and beat those big 'uns.

Offense sells tickets. Defense wins games.

More football games are lost than won.

❖

Don't talk too much or too soon.

❖

Winning isn't the only thing, but it beats whatever comes in second.
                                        −Sign in Bryant's office

❖

One of the greatest things Coach Bryant used to do was pass along the credit.
                    −Gene Stallings, who played for Bryant, coached for Bryant,
                                and followed him as head coach at Alabama

My favorite play is the one where our player pitches the ball back to the official after scoring a touchdown.

The biggest mistake coaches make is taking borderline cases and trying to save them. I'm not talking about grades, I'm talking about character. I want to know before a boy enrolls about his home life, and what his parents want him to be.

The Ballcarrier
Author Unknown

My boy, when the fight is the grimmest,
And it seems that you cannot gain,
And you've hurtled yourself at the steel-like line
Again, and again and again,
And the tackle rebuffs your plunges,
And the ends are as swift as light,
And you've started to doubt your power,
Right then is the time to fight.
You feel that you're shot to pieces;
Ah, lad, but someday you'll know,
That the battles of life and football,
Are won by the final blow.
For the ones who have hit the hardest,
Are as weakened, my boy, as you,
And the fight must come down to courage,
The last vital drop or two.
So buck up your heart, young fellow,
And though all the heavens may fall,
Give 'em your heart-core wallop,
The next time you carry the ball.
And I'll tell you, dear boy, the heroes,
Who watch from their heights will say,
"There's a lad with a winner's courage;
Make way for a man, make way…"

Hugh "Duffy" Daugherty
Michigan State

Born: Emeigh, Pennsylvania
College: Syracuse, 1940
Coached: Michigan State
Years: 18
Record: 109-69-5
Accomplishments:
- 4 national championships
- 2 Big Ten championships
- 10-7-2 vs. Michigan
- 10-7-7 vs Notre Dame

Beating the University of Michigan is not a matter of life or death.
It's more important than that.

It's been said football is a contact sport. Not so! Football is a collision sport; dancing is a contact sport.

The best way to better your lot is to do a lot better.

The harder you work the luckier you get.

He can run and he can pass, he can kick, play offense or defense. He has only one weakness…. He's a senior.

> – Daugherty, regarding All-American Sherm Lewis

The difference between good and great is just a little extra effort.

Anybody can carry a football. It's just some guys can carry it farther and faster.

I like goal line stands. I wish our defense would do them up around the 50 yard line so I could see them better.

Some men are bigger, faster, stronger, and smarter than others—but not a single man has a corner on dreams, desire, or ambition.

Only three things can happen when you throw the football—and two of them are bad.

We like them big at Michigan State. But we'll settle for players with three kinds of bones—a funny bone, a wishbone, and a back bone. The funny bone is to enjoy a laugh, even at one's own expense. The wishbone is to think big, set one's goals high, and to have dreams and ambitions. And the backbone—well, that's what a boy needs to get up and go to work and make all his dreams come true.

Anonymous alum in a telegram to Duffy Daugherty shortly before a big game:
Remember, Coach, we're behind you 100%—win or tie.

One of Daugherty's favorites:
For when that One Great Scorer comes to mark against your name,
He writes—not that you won or lost—but how you played the game.
                                                    —Grantland Rice, sportswriter

If you get caught up in things you have no control over it will affect adversely the things you do have control over.

It's All in a State of Mind
Walter D. Wintle

If you think you are beaten, you are;
If you think you dare not, you won't;
If you like to win, but don't think you can,
It's almost a cinch you won't.
If you think you'll lose, you've lost;
For out in the world you'll find success
Success begins with a fellow's will,
It's all in a state of mind.

For many a game is lost ere even a play is run,
And many a coward fails before his work is begun.
Think big and your deeds will grow,
Think small and you'll fall behind;
Think that you can and you will;
It's all in a state of mind.

If you think you are out-classed you are;
You've got to think high to rise;
You've got to be sure of yourself,
Before you can win the prize.
Life's battles don't always go,
To the stronger or faster man,
But sooner or later, the man who wins,
Is the fellow who thinks he can.

Your success depends upon you. You have to steer your own course. You have to do your own thing. You must make your own decisions. You have to solve your own problems. Your character is your handiwork. You have to write your own record. You have to build your own monument—or dig your own pit. Which are you doing?

—B.C. Forbes

Bob Devaney
Nebraska

Born: Big Beaver, Michigan
College: Alma College, 1939
Coached: Wyoming, Nebraska
Years: 16
Record: 136-30-7
Accomplishments:
- 8 Big Eight championships
- 2 national championships
- 10 bowl Games
- Devaney's 1971 Nebraska team has been called by many the best college football team of all time.

I don't expect to win enough games to be put on NCAA probation. I just want to win enough to warrant an investigation.

—Devaney, upon being hired at Nebraska

I cannot give you a formula for success, but I can give you the formula for failure: try to please everybody.

To get a true measure of a player or coach, note how much more he does than is required of him.

How about instead of loving your enemies, treat your teammates a little better.

I had a friend with a lifetime contract. After two bad years, the university president called him into his office and pronounced him dead.

—Devaney, on why he didn't seek a lifetime contract

Goals achieved with little effort are seldom appreciated and give no personal satisfaction.

❖

It is amazing how much can be accomplished if no one cares who gets the credit.

❖

Don't overcelebrate in the end zone. Act like you knew you were going to get there.

❖

The Only Way to Win
Author Unknown

It takes a little courage,
And a little self-control,
And some grim determination,
If you want to reach your goal.
It takes some real striving,
And a firm and stern-set chin,
No matter what the battle,
If you really want to win.

There's no easy path to glory,
There's no rosy road to fame,
Life, however we may view it,
Is no simple parlor game.
But its prizes call for fighting,
For endurance and for grit,
For a rugged disposition,
And a "don't-know-when-to-quit."

You must take a blow or give one.
You must risk and you must lose,
And expect that in the struggle,
You will suffer from the bruise.
But you must not wince or falter,
If a fight you once begin;
Be a man and face the battle—
That's the only way to win.

How to be a Champion
Grantland Rice

You wonder how they do it,
And you look to see the knack,
You watch the foot in action,
Or the shoulder, or the back.
But when you spot the answer,
Where the higher glamours lurk,
The most of it is practice,
And the rest of it is work.

Positive Attitude
Anonymous (Locker Room)

Having a positive mental attitude is developing an image of yourself as a winning athlete. To accomplish this, you must:
- acquire the skills required by your position;
- improve on those skills with your hours of practice;
- get yourself into peak physical condition, and
- achieve some success which will encourage you to work even harder

Thus, the cycle includes learning, working, and succeeding. Then, because you enjoy the success, you'll learn more, work more, and succeed more.

To win, you must act as if it were impossible to fail. If you expect the best, you will get the best. If you expect the worst, you'll probably get the worst.

There are always two ways to look at everything that happens to you—the positive way or the negative way. The negative person even discounts the good things that happen to him by calling them lucky. The positive person refuses to accept a defeat or a problem as something bad. He treats defeat as a learning process and problems as challenges.

Don't be susceptible to the negative influence of other people. You will have people telling you your entire life what you can't do. You show them what you can do. Don't let yourself be dragged down by their negative thoughts, words, and actions. Negative attitudes are contagious, but so too are positive attitudes. Have a positive attitude—look for the best in other people and the best in every situation. Let others catch your attitude.

Bobby Dodd
Georgia Tech

Born: Galax, Virginia
College: Tennessee, 1931
Coached: Georgia Tech
Years: 22
Record: 165-64-8
Accomplishments:
- As Tennessee quarterback, Dodd led the team to a 27-1-2 record
- 13 bowl games (8 straight victories)
- 1 national championship
- Dodd is 1 of only 2 men enshrined in the College Football Hall of Fame both as a coach and player. The other is A.A. Stagg.

When the Pressure's On
Author Unknown

How do you act when the pressure's on,
When the chance for victory's almost gone,
When Fortune's star has refused to shine,
When the ball is on your five-yard line?
How do you act when the going's rough,
Does your spirit lag when breaks are tough?
Or, is there in you a flame that glows,
Brighter as fiercer the battle grows?
How hard, how long will you fight the foe?
That's what the world would like to know!
Cowards can fight when they're out ahead!
The uphill grind shows a thoroughbred!
You wish for success?—Then tell me, son,
How do you act when the pressure's on?

If you think you're lucky, you are.

Either love your players or get out of coaching.

The big game of next week, month, or year is being won or lost right now.

He taught us to care because he cared. He taught us to be concerned because he was concerned. He taught us that honesty is sacred, is absolute, and is eternal.

–Frank Broyles, player and assistant coach for Dodd

ABC's to Achieve Your Dreams
Anonymous

Avoid negative people, places, things, and habits.
Believe in yourself.
Consider things from every side.
Don't give up, and don't give in.
Enjoy life today; yesterday is past, and tomorrow is not yet.
Family and friends are hidden treasures. Seek them and enjoy their riches.
Give more than you planned to give.
Hang on to your dreams.
Ignore those who try to discourage you.
Just do it; and do it now!
Keep on trying. No matter how hard it seems, it will get easier.
Love yourself first and most.
Make something happen. Who else will?
Never lie, cheat, or steal.
Open your eyes, and see things as they really are.
Practice, practice, practice…
Quitters never win, and winners never quit.
Resolve to reflect on your life experiences.
Slow down, pay attention.
Take control of your own destiny.
Understand yourself in order to better understand others.
Visualize it first.
Waste not your opportunities.
E**X**amine for what you are exchanging one day of your life.
You are unique of all God's creations. Nothing nor nobody can replace you.
Zip the lip more often.

Vince Dooley
Georgia

Born: Mobile, Alabama
College: Auburn, 1954
Coached: University of Georgia
Years: 25
Record: 201-77-10
Accomplishments:
- 20 bowl games
- 1 national championship
- 6 SEC championships

The Great Competitor
Grantland Rice

Beyond the winning and the goal,
Beyond the glory and the fame,
He feels the flame within his soul,
Born of the spirit of the game.
And where the barriers may wait,
Built up by the opposing gods,
He finds a thrill in bucking fate,
And riding down the odds.
He finds a new and deeper thrill,
To take him on the uphill spin.
Because the test is greater still,
And something he can revel in.

To err is human, to forgive is divine. But to forgive a football coach is unheard of.

Keep team rules to a minimum. But enforce the ones you have.

There are two kinds of discipline: self-discipline and team discipline. You need both.

You've got to do everything well, but you've got to play defense first.

Pat Dye
Auburn

Born: Augusta, Georgia
College: Georgia
Coached: East Carolina, Wyoming, Auburn
Years: 18
Record: 153-62-5
Accomplishments:
- 10 bowl games
- 4 SEC championships

Nothing has changed about what makes a winner. A winner works his butt off and is dependable. He's not always the most talented, but he gives everything on every play.

If you're a football coach, criticism comes with the territory. If it tears you up, you better get into another profession.

Life is short, so don't waste any of it carrying around a load of bitterness. It only sours your life, and the world won't pay any attention anyway.

—Dye, to the press after being fired

Keep football a tough sport that teaches men to think, to dare, to hit hard, to lead, to sacrifice, to fight, to win, and to disdain the tie or defeat. College football is the greatest game man plays. Protect it well. Keep it a tough sport and a teacher of men. College football is the greatest game man plays. Gentlemen … *protect it well!*

—Dan Jessee, coach, Trinity College, to the American Football Coaches Association

Hayden Fry

Iowa

Born: Eastland, Texas
College: Baylor, 1951
Coached: SMU, North Texas, Iowa
Years: 37
Record: 232-178-10
Accomplishments:
- 15 bowl games
- 3 Big Ten Championships
- 4th in all-time Big 10 victories
- 11 seasons with 10 or more wins

People hit only what they aim at...so aim high.

In business, family, football, and life, scratch where it itches. And if it ain't broke don't try and fix it.

All great athletes turn on their own motor and control their own emotions. It's the other guys on the team you have to worry about.

Master the fundamentals, then you have a chance to win.

Think before you do anything. Ask yourself, "Will it help us win?" If it won't, don't do it.

Talent is God-given; be humble.
Fame is man-given; be thankful.
Conceit is self-given; be careful.

When you got something going good, squeeze it till it's dry.

The sun don't shine on the same hound dog's rump everyday.

What Is a Competitor?
Raymond Berry, Hall of Fame receiver, Baltimore Colts

He plays like every play means the championship. The guy never gives up. He's never beat mentally. He's a game player. He comes through for the team. He is consistent. He does his job every play. Setbacks don't discourage him. He's never satisfied with his performance. He keeps on going play after play—*full speed*. He runs you to death. You can't relax for a moment. He doesn't play cautious. He's aggressive—always on the attack. He's more interested in the team than personal glory and winning is the most important goal.

I believe life is constantly testing us for our level of commitment, and life's greatest rewards are reserved for those who demonstrate a never-ending commitment to act until they achieve. This level of resolve can move mountains, but it must be constant and consistent. As simplistic as this may sound, it is still the common denominator separating those who live their dreams from those who live in regret.

–Anthony Robbins

Until one is committed, there is hesitancy, the chance to draw back, always ineffectiveness. Concerning all acts of initiative and creation, there is one elementary truth, the ignorance of which kills countless ideas and splendid plans: that the moment one definitely commits oneself, then providence moves too. All sorts of things occur to help one that would never otherwise have occurred. A whole stream of events issues from the decision, raising in one's favor all manner of unforeseen incidents, meetings, and material assistance which no man could have dreamed would have come his way. Whatever you can do or dream you can, begin it. Boldness has genius, power and magic in it. Begin it now.

–Goethe

Yup, you prove it every day you overthrow your wide-open receivers.
–Fry, when a backup quarterback told him
he had a better arm than the starter

Stick It Out

Author Unknown

When your world's about to fall,
And your back's against the wall,
When you're facing wild retreat and utter rout;
When it seems that naught can stop it,
All your pleas and plans can't prop it,
Get a grip upon yourself and—stick it out!

Any craven fool can quit,
But a man with pluck and grit,
Will hold until the very final shout;
In the snarling teeth of sorrow,
He will laugh and say, "Tomorrow,
The luck will change—I guess I'll stick it out."

The luck does change; you know it,
All the records prove and show it,
And the men who win are men who strangle doubt,
Who do not hesitate nor swerve,
Who have grit and guts and nerve,
And whose motto is: Play hard, and stick it out.

And you think you can't last long,
When things begin to go wrong,
That you've got to quit, not wait for the final bout;
Just smile at your beholders,
Clench your teeth and square your shoulders
You'll win if you but fight and *stick it out!*

So You Had a Bad Day

Robert Service

You're sick of the game, why, that's a shame; you're young, you're brave, and you're bright. You have had a raw deal, I know, but don't squeal, buck up! Do your darndest and fight! It's the plugging away that will win you the day. So don't be a piker 'ole pard; just call on your grit, it's so easy to quit. It's keeping on living that's hard.

It's easy to cry that you're beaten, and die. It's easy to crawfish and crawl, but to fight and to fight when hope's out of sight, why, that's the best game of them all. And although you come out of each grueling bout all broken and beaten and scarred, just give one more try; it's so easy to die, it's keeping your chin up that's hard.

Alonzo Smith "Jake" Gaither
Florida A&M

Born: Dayton, Tennessee
College: Knoxville College, TN
Coached: Florida A&M
Years: 25
Record: 203-36-4
Accomplishments:
- 6 Black College national titles
- 23 Southern Intercollegiate championships
- 12 one-loss seasons
- 3 undefeated seasons

I want my boys ag-ile, mo-bile, and hos-tile.

Excuses are no good. Your friends don't need them, and your enemies won't believe them.

I never watched an athlete become a champion that I didn't smell sweat.

It's bad coaching to blame your boys for losing a game, even if it's true.

Never leave the field with a boy feeling you're mad at him. You can chew him out on the field, but then pat him on the shoulder in the locker room.

Whether he likes it or not, each man has got to cut if for himself. He can't blame the referee or the coach or the opposing players. He finds out about himself very quickly on the field. Where else do they become men quicker than on a football field? Somewhere along the line he's going to face the ultimate test, and he'll know right away if he has succeeded or not.

A thoroughbred responds to the whip. A jackass bucks, sits down, and cries.

Joe Gibbs
Washington Redskins

Active

Born: Mocksville, North Carolina
College: San Diego State, 1963
Coached: Washington Redskins
Years: 12 (retired in 1993, returned in 2004)
Record: 140-65
Accomplishments:
- 5 division championships
- 4 Super Bowls (3-1) with 3 different quarterbacks
- 8 playoff appearances
- 10th all-time NFL victories

So You're Thinking about Getting Out!
Author Unknown

So you have some doubts about coaching, about whether or not it's worth it. Sometimes the road looks too long and too tough, and you feel like quitting. You wonder if you have the determination and the energy to go through another season.

Well, take an honest look at yourself. You weren't very well-prepared when you started, and you made countless mistakes that cost plenty. Often you were guilty of looking for short cuts, of trying to find an easy way, when you knew very well there was no such thing.

Over the years you've been ridiculed, humiliated, and treated unfairly by all kinds of people. Often your work has gone unappreciated. You've been broke. You've been tired. And you've been afraid of being fired. It's tough. And it will never get any easier unless you decide to take the easy way out—which is all the way out, quitting.

You may not have realized it, but from the very beginning you were destined to be a coach. You think of all the days and all the dreams that have gone into making you what you are. Other than your family and your God, what else has ever really mattered to you? There's important work to be done—*and you can do it!*

Look for players with character and ability. But remember, character comes first.

To win it all, a team has to be obsessive about the fundamentals and the little things.

What my wife Pat was taking care of at home was far more important than what I was taking care of with the Washington Redskins.

Striving for happiness through achievement should not be a goal. If it is, you'll never reach it.

The credit belongs to the man who is actually in the arena; whose fate is marred by dust and sweat and blood; who errs and comes up short again; who knows great enthusiasm and great devotion, and spends himself in a worthy cause; who at best knows in the end the triumph of high achievement; and who at the worst, if he fails, at least fails while daring greatly; so that his place shall never be with those cold and timid souls who know neither victory nor defeat.

–Theodore Roosevelt, President of the United States

In football as in life, it's sometimes fourth-and-one.
And there are those urging us to go for it.

The lessons in my life have come from failures, my own shortcomings, naiveté, and buying into some of the biggest myths modern society has to sell.

The only way to please the world is win every time. That isn't the case with God. God loves us more when we're having a tough time than when we are winning.

Failures are expected by losers, ignored by winners.

I expect peak performance from myself, my staff, and my players.
Sometimes you lose anyway.

We Need Coaches
Author Unknown

...who cannot be bought.

...whose word is their bond.

...who put character above wealth.

...who possess opinions and a will.

...who are larger than their vocations.

...who do not hesitate to take chances.

...who will make no compromise with wrong.

...who will not lose their individuality in a crowd.

...who will be as honest in small things as in great things.

...who will not say I did it "because everybody else does it."

...whose ambitions are not confined to their own selfish desires.

...who give thirty-six inches to the yard and thirty-two quarts to the bushel.

...who will not have one brand of honesty for football purposes and another for private life.

...who are true to their friends through good report and bad report, in adversity as well as in prosperity.

...who do not believe that shrewdness, sharpness, cunning, and strong-headedness are the best qualities for winning success.

...who are not ashamed or afraid to stand for the truth when it is unpopular

...who can say "No" with emphasis, although all the rest of the world says "Yes."

A Philosophy of Life
Thomas Jefferson

In matters of principle, stand like a rock; in matters of taste, swim with the current. Give up money, give up fame, give up science, give up the earth itself and all it contains, rather than do an immoral act. And never suppose, that in any possible situation, or under any circumstances, it is best for you to do a dishonorable thing. Whenever you are to do a thing, though it can never be known but to yourself, ask yourself how you would act were all the world looking at you, and act accordingly.

He who permits himself to tell a lie once finds it much easier to do it a second and third time, till at length it becomes habitual; he tells a lie without attending to it, and truths without the world believing him.

Why Coach

Tiger Ellison

(Legendary high school coach in Ohio and assistant to Woody Hayes at Ohio State, from a speech before the National Football Coaches Association)

An old man going a lone highway,
Came at evening cold and gray,
To a chasm vast and wide,
Through which was flowing a swollen tide.
The old man crossed in the twilight dim,
That swollen stream held no fears for him,
But he paused when safe on the other side,
And built a bridge to span the tide.
"Old man," said a fellow pilgrim near,
"You are wasting your strength with building here.
Your journey will end with the ending day;
You never again must pass this way.
You have crossed the chasm deep and wide;
Why build you the bridge at the eventide?"
The builder lifted his old gray head
"In the path that I have come," he said,
"There followed after me today,
A youth whose feet must pass this way.
This swollen stream which was naught to me,
To that fair-haired youth may a pitfall be.
He, too, must cross in the twilight dim.
Good friend, I am building the bridge for him."

This Is My Team

It is composed of people like me—we make it what it is. It will be friendly—if I am. It will have a good attitude—if I have a good attitude. It will do great work—if I work. It will be disciplined—if I am disciplined. It will be a team filled with love and loyalty—if I help to fill it with these. Therefore, with the help of God, I shall dedicate myself to the task of being all the things I want my team to be.

Wayne Woodrow "Woody" Hayes
Ohio State

Born: Clifton, Ohio
College: Denison University, Ohio
Coached: Denison, Miami of Ohio, Ohio State
Years: 33
Record: 238-72-10
Accomplishments:
- 13 Big Ten championships
- 5 national championships
- 11 bowl games
- 8 Rose Bowls (4 consecutive)
- 56 First-Team All-Americans

Indomitable in defeat, insufferable in victory.
—A Big Ten president, on Hayes

They may outsmart me, or be luckier, but they can't out work me.

Woody loves to brag about how many of his players get their diplomas. Let the liberals talk about football factories and jocks. Why, he can teach a boy more in two months than some of those professors do in four years.
—Faculty representative at a Big Ten rival

I'd rather have a loyal assistant coach than a brilliant one.

It worries me that there's supposed to be a coach meaner than I am. I would hate to have them start referring to me as "Good Old Woody."

He was a great coach but he was an even better man.
—Archie Griffin, Ohio State All-American and 2-time Heisman Trophy winner

If it comes easy, it ain't worth a damn.

My golf game reminds me of Woody Hayes, and Ohio State. Three yards and a cloud of dust.

–Bill Dooley, coach, Virginia Tech

I recruited a Czech kicker, and during the eye examination the doc asked if he could read the bottom line. The Czech kicker said, "Read it! I know him!"

Without winners there could be no civilization.

You don't get hurt running straight at them for 3 yards and a cloud of dust. I will pound you and pound you and pound you until you quit.

Hayes' 10 Virtues and Characteristics of a Good Leader

- Positive image, character, and integrity
- Mental toughness, to endure and rebound
- Communication skills
- Understanding the role of the leader
- Know your limits and be yourself
- Preparation, including anticipation
- Accessibility and visibility
- Confidence
- Ability to initiate interaction
- Realize the spiritual power of people

Any time you give a man something he doesn't earn, you cheapen him. Our kids earn what they get, and that includes respect.

Luck is infatuated with the efficient

—Persian proverb

Chance favors the prepared mind.

—Louis Pasteur

If I don't practice for one day, I know it; if I don't practice for two days, the *critics* know it; if I don't practice for three days, everyone knows it.

—Ignace Paderewski, the great Polish pianist

The will to win is not nearly as important as the will to prepare to win.

—Anonymous

Proper preparation prevents poor performance.

—U.S. Marines

Plan your work and work your plan.

—U.S. Army

Leaders without followers are impotent;
Leaders with talentless followers are ineffective.
You win with good people.

—Hayes, on recruiting

❖

Hayes, to a professor at Ohio State who was a critic: Remember, I can do your job but you can't do mine.

❖

Paralyze their resistance with persistence.

Old Woody isn't trying to win a popularity contest, I'm trying to win football games. I don't like sweet, sugary, nice people. I like tough, hardworking, honest people.

In football there is no room for self-pity or feeling sorry for yourself. You just get up, dust yourself off, and try harder.

Anne Hayes, Woody's wife, in response to a heckler who said "Your husband is a fathead!": What husband isn't?

Victories come about by simplicity not complexity; by solidity not experimentation; by dedication not imagination.

Hayes' natural law of college football: The direct mathematical relation between victories and alumni donations.

You cannot afford ever to feel sorry for yourself. Feeling sorry is what leads to alcohol and drugs. And those things tear you apart.

Always tell your team, other teams can't beat us. We beat ourselves by not being in condition, having dissension, not being prepared, not paying attention to fundamentals—blocking, tackling—missing assignments, fumbling, throwing interceptions, getting fatheaded. That's how you lose. Let the other guy beat himself.

John Heisman
Georgia Tech

Born: Cleveland, Ohio
College: Brown, 1890
Coached: Oberlin, Akron, Auburn, Clemson, Georgia Tech,
  Pennsylvania, Washington & Jefferson, Rice
Years: 36
Record: 185-70-17
Accomplishments:
  - The Heisman Trophy, which goes to college football's best player, is named after John Heisman.
  - His Georgia Tech team beat Cumberland 222-0. In 1918, he beat Furman 118-0, the 11th Cavalry 123-0, and North Carolina State 128-0.

Coaches should be masterful, commanding, even dictatorial. A coach has no time to say "please" or "mister." Occasionally, he must be severe.

When in doubt, punt!

To Sportsmen Who Love the Game
Grantland Rice

To sportsmen who love the game beyond all profit and fame.
I lift my glass. Here's to the creed of you.
Here's to the breed of you.
Here while the bugles call.
Here, where we rise and fall.
Here, where we storm the wall, you paved the way.
Oh where the cannons roar,
Knowing the heart calls for,
You wrote the winning score
Back in our day.

Luck is always against the man who depends on it.

When you find your opponent's weak spot, hammer it.

What is it? It is a prolate spheroid—that is, an elongated sphere—in which the outer leather casing is drawn tightly over a somewhat small rubber tubing. Better to have died a small boy than for any of you to fumble it.
     –Heisman, on the first day of practice each year, while holding up a football

❖

Great truth is simple, so also are great coaches.

❖

Food for Thought
Author Unknown

I watched them tearing a building down,
A gang of men in a busy town,
With a ho-heave-ho and a lusty yell,
They swung a beam and the sidewall fell.
I asked the foremen, Are these men as skilled
as the men you'd hire if you had to build?
He gave a laugh and said, No indeed,
Just common labor is all I need.
I can easily wreck in a day or two,
What builders have taken a year to do!
And I thought to myself as I went my way,
Which of these roles have I tried to play?
Am I a builder who works with care,
Measuring life by the rule and square?
Am I shaping my deeds to a well-made plan,
Patiently doing the best I can?
Or am I a wrecker who walks the town,
Content with the labor of tearing down.

There is a choice you make in everything you do, and you must remember the choice you make, makes you. Don't cuss, don't argue with the officials, and don't lose the game.

❖

One of the rarest things that a man ever does is the very best he can….

❖

Commitment to Excellence
Anonymous

How good do you want to be? If your answer is, "good enough to get by," then a commitment to excellence is not necessary. But if your completely honest answer is, "the best," you must make a total commitment to excellence.

You don't have to tell anyone about your commitment, because actions speak louder than words. People will see your commitment in the time you put into practicing and the way you practice.

Never be ashamed to admit that you want to be the best and never feel you should have to explain why you want to be the best. Your answer should be, "Why not the best?" Don't be satisfied until you get what you want.

In my many years of coaching, I have seen a dozen or so young athletes make a sincere commitment to excellence. They had the burning desire to be not just good, but great. They craved coaching. They went out of their way to look for tougher competition. Finally, they were very stubborn—they refused to settle for anything less than the best.

As a result, each was a big winner. There was no luck or chance involved; they worked hard so they would always have an edge when they went into each game. They knew that they would win… and they did.

Perfection is very elusive. There are always ways to improve. In striving for perfection, though, you do accomplish things that you might not accomplish without a commitment to excellence.

I often wonder how people can be at peace with themselves or totally happy when they have not made such a commitment. How do they justify their lives—how do they go day after day without making an honest effort to be the best at what they do? It's up to you. If you refuse to settle for less than the best, you'll probably become the best.

Lou Holtz
South Carolina

Active

Born: Follansbee, West Virginia
College: Kent State, 1959
Coached: William and Mary, North Carolina State, Arkansas,
    Minnesota, Notre Dame, South Carolina
Years: 33
Record: 243-137-7
Accomplishments:
- 23 bowl games
- 1 national championship
- Won 100 games in 11 years at Notre Dame
- Led 6 different programs to bowl games
- Led 4 programs to top 20 rankings

I can't believe God put us on this earth to be ordinary.

You know, whether it's in business, politics, education, or athletics, there has to be respect and loyalty for the leader. Success depends on it. There are three questions from the leader that must be answered affirmatively by individual group members if the group needs assurance that it can reach its desired goal. Can I trust you? Are you committed? Do you respect or care about me? If the individuals can answer "yes" to their leader to these three questions, even greatness is within their grasp.

One day you are drinking wine, and the next day you're picking the grapes.

Don't ever ask a player to do something he doesn't have the ability to do, because he'll question your ability to coach.

My father-in-law and I have a great deal in common. We both love football, golf, and his daughter, but not necessarily in that order.

You live up—or down—to your expectations.

Coaching is nothing more than eliminating mistakes before you get fired.

❖

Anytime your defense gives up more points than your basketball team, you're in trouble.

❖

Too many times we love what we don't have and it keeps us from using what we do have.

❖

Nothing is as bad as it seems and nothing is as good as it seems. Reality is somewhere in between.

❖

Self-discipline is an individual's greatest asset.

❖

The man who complains about the way the ball bounces is usually the one who dropped it.

❖

When all is said and done, more is said than done.

❖

I will not accept anything less than the best a player's capable of doing, and he has the right to expect the best that I can do for him and the team.

❖

Motivation is simple. Just eliminate those who aren't motivated.

❖

Don't be a spectator. Don't let life pass you by.

❖

Praise loudly. Criticize softly.

If you don't make a total commitment to whatever you're doing, then you start looking to bail out the first time the boat starts leaking. It's tough enough getting that boat to shore with everybody rowing, let alone when some guy stands up and starts putting his life jacket on.

❖

The only important thing about the time of possession is who gets to keep the ball after the game is over.

❖

I don't know what the future holds but I sure know who holds the future.

❖

Our guidelines require players to arrive promptly for practice and meetings, obey their coaches, maintain certain academic standards, and conduct themselves with dignity. We ask them to behave like responsible adults. Do what is right and avoid what is wrong.

❖

Never be afraid to demand excellence.

❖

Leaders are obligated to bring out the best in their people.

❖

Never bet against anyone who is committed to excellence.

❖

I never punished anyone; the offenders chose the punishment themselves by their actions.

❖

Players create their future; it doesn't exist until they decide what it should be.

❖

People don't care how much you know until they know how much you care.

Ability is what you are capable of doing. Motivation determines what you do. Attitude determines how well you do it.

❖

Concentrate on the word *win*: What's Important Now.

❖

Winners or losers are not born; they are the product of how they think.

❖

You will succumb to stress if you are ill-prepared.

❖

A man is not finished when he is defeated. He is finished when he quits. No matter how many times you are knocked down, you get off the floor even if you are bloody, battered, beaten. Just keep getting up.

❖

All That I Ask
Author Unknown

Give me men who will run with abandon.
Give me men who will tackle and block.
Give me men who are rough, tough and nasty,
And growl like a bear when they walk.
Give me men who are conscious of spirit.
Give me men with great fortitude.
Give me men who will play for the love
of the team, an all for one attitude.
Give me men who will fight for survival.
Give me men who will face any task.
Give me men who when molded together,
Make a team, that's all that I ask.
Give me these men, I will take them,
night and day I will work with a grin.
I'll teach them the techniques of football,
and I'll give you a team that will win!

If you have something you believe in, and it's worth fighting for, the greatest test is not when you are standing, but when you are down. Study leaders in history, those admired most are those who have gone through adversity and come back. You've got to learn to survive a defeat. That's when you develop real character.

—Author Unknown

Believe in Yourself and Make It Possible, Not Easy
Pete McCulley

Believe in yourself—not only on the days when the going is great and you are winning and nothing seems impossible, but on days when the whole world looks lousy and you are losing, and the road ahead looks difficult, and you wonder if you are brave enough, smart enough, strong enough, or insane enough to try.

Refuse to quit, not now and not ever. Keep believing in yourself, no matter how many people discourage you, doubt you, laugh at you, warn you, or think you a fool. Never listen to the voice of another, only the one deep inside of you saying, "You can do it and you will." If no one else in the world gives a darn or believes in you, believe in yourself.

There will be times when you doubt your own ability, feel discouraged, and on the verge of despair. Don't even consider the possibility of giving up . Hang on and fan the fire that burns deep inside.

Load your own coal and warm yourself twice, once from the exercise and once from the furnace.

Tom Landry
Dallas Cowboys

Born: Mission, Texas
College: Texas 1949
Coached: Dallas Cowboys
Years: 29
Record: 270-178-6
Accomplishments:

- All-Pro defensive back with the New York Giants
- 20 consecutive winning seasons
- 18 playoff appearances
- 13 division championships
- 5 NFC titles
- 5 Super Bowl appearances
- 2 Super Bowl championships

He's a perfectionist. If he was married to Raquel Welch, he'd expect her to cook.

—Don Meredith, former Cowboy quarterback

Coach Landry's priorities in life became my priorities. His players are his legacy. We will pass him on to our children and nation.

—Bob Lilly, Cowboy All-Pro defensive tackle

Motivation should come from within, not from the head coach.

When you want to win a game, you teach. When you lose a game, you better learn.

To get men to do what they don't want to do in order to achieve what they want to achieve. That's what coaching is all about.

❖

Public relations is great, but there's no public relations like winning.

Walt Garrison, former Cowboys fullback, when asked if Landry ever smiles: I don't know. I only played there nine years.

I really don't have a goal to be the greatest coach in the business. I just try to achieve the best with the talent God has given me. If I do that, I'm satisfied.

Leadership is a matter of having people look at you and gain confidence, seeing how you react. If you're in control they're in control.

The secret to winning is constant, consistent management.

What really counts is not the number of hours you put in,
But how much you put in the hours.

I remember an epitaph which is in the cemetery at Tombstone, Arizona. It says: "Here lies Jack Williams. He done his damnedest." I think that is the greatest epitaph a man can have. When a man gives everything that is in him to do the job he has before him. That is all you can ask of him and that is what I have tried to do.
—Harry S. Truman, President of the United States

Never discourage anyone who continually makes progress, no matter how slow.
—Plato

My code of life and conduct is simply this: work hard; play to the allowable limit; disregard equally the good and bad opinion of others; never do a friend a dirty trick; never grow indignant over anything; live the moment to the utmost of its possibilities; and be satisfied with life always, but never with oneself.
—George Jean Nathan

Most of the athletes who fail to become winners are those athletes whose fears and anxieties prevent them from reaching their potential. I overcame my fears and anxieties by a commitment to something far greater than winning a football game—a commitment to Jesus Christ.

Apostle Paul explained my discovery in I Corinthians 9:24-27 better than I can:

"In a race, everyone runs, but only one person gets first prize. So run your race to win. To win the contest, you must deny yourselves many things that would keep you from doing your best. An athlete goes to all this trouble just to win a ribbon or a silver cup, but we do it for a heavenly reward that never disappears. So I run straight to the goal with purpose in every step. I fight to win. I am not just shadowboxing or playing around. Like an athlete, I punish my body, treating it roughly, training it to do what it should, not what it wants to. Otherwise, I fear that after enlisting others for the race, I myself might be declared unfit and ordered to stand aside."

You have got to have courage. I don't care how good a man is, if he is timid, his value is limited. The timid will not amount to very much in this world. I want to see a good man ready to smite with the sword. I want to see him able to hold his own in active life against the force of evil.
—Theodore Roosevelt, President of the United States

In matters of principle, stand like a rock; in matters of taste, swim with the current. Give up money, give up fame, give up science, give up the earth itself and all it contains, rather than do an immoral act. And never suppose, that in any possible situation, or under any circumstances, it is best for you to do a dishonorable thing. Whenever you are to do a thing, though it can never be known but to yourself, ask yourself how would you act were all the world looking at you, and act accordingly.

He who permits himself to tell a lie once finds it much easier to do it a second and third time, till at length it becomes habitual; he tells a lie without attending to it, and truths without the world believing him.
—Thomas Jefferson, President of the United States

Vince Lombardi
Green Bay Packers

Born: Brooklyn, New York
College: Fordham, 1938
Coached: Green Bay, Washington
Years: 10
Record: 141-39-4
Accomplishments:
- Member of the Fordham front line known as the "Seven Blocks of Granite"
- 5 NFL championships
- 2 AFL-NFL Super Bowl championships
- 1 Western Division championship

He treats us all the same…like dogs.
> –Henry Jordan, Green Bay Packer defensive tackle, on Lombardi's fairness

Leaders are made, they are not born. They are made by hard effort, which is the price which all of us must pay to achieve any goal that is worthwhile.

Some people try to find things in this game or put things into it which don't exist. Football is two things. It's blocking and tackling. I don't care anything about formations or new offenses or tricks on defense. You block and tackle better than the team you're playing, you win.

You must recognize what has to be done, and then try to do it. It's a matter of recognition, adjustment, and execution, in that order.

To achieve success, whatever the job, we must pay a price. Anything worthwhile has a price. You have to pay the price to get to the point where success is possible.

Physical strength will make the opponent weaken and mental toughness will make him crack.

Having the capacity to lead is not enough. The leader must be willing to use it. His leadership is then based on truth and character. There must be truth in the purpose and willpower in the character.

Commitment to Excellence

I owe most everything in my life to football. I have never lost my respect, my admiration, or my love for what I consider a great game. Each Sunday, after the battle, one group savors victory, another group lives in the bitterness of defeat. The many hurts seem a small price to have paid for having won, and there is no reason at all that is adequate for having lost. It's a game, I think, a great deal like life in that it demands that a man's personal commitment be toward victory. Each week there's a new encounter, each year a new challenge. All of the rings and all of the money and all of the color and all of the display linger only in memory. The spirit, the will to win, and the will to excel, these are the things that endure and these are the qualities that are so much more important than any of the events that occasion them. I would like to say that the quality of any man's life has got to be that man's personal commitment to excellence and to victory, regardless of what field he may be in.

Mental toughness is many things and rather difficult to explain. Its qualities are sacrifice and self-denial. Also, most importantly, it is combined with a perfectly disciplined will that refuses to give in. It's a state of mind—you could call it character in action.

Football is like life—it requires perseverance, self denial, hard work, sacrifice, dedication, and respect for authority.

Unless a man believes in himself and makes a total commitment to his career and puts everything he has into it—his mind, his body and his heart—what is life worth to him? If I were a salesman, I would make this commitment to my company, to the product, and most of all, to myself.

Once you have established the goals you want and the price you're willing to pay, you can ignore the minor hurts, the opponent's pressure, and temporary failures.

A man can be as great as he wants to be. If you believe in yourself and have the courage, the determination, the dedication, the competitive drive, and if you are willing to sacrifice the little things in life and pay the price for the things that are worthwhile, it can be done.

Small hurts are a part of football as well as a part of life.

It's easy to have faith in yourself and have discipline when you're a winner, when you're number one. What you've got to have is faith and discipline when you're not yet a winner.

People who work together will win, whether it be against complex football defenses, or the problems of modern society.

If you'll not settle for anything less than your best, you will be amazed at what you can accomplish in your lives.

Build for your team a feeling of oneness, of dependence upon one another, and of strength to be derived by unity.

The difference between a successful person and others is not a lack of knowledge, but rather in a lack of will.

It is essential to understand that battles are primarily won in the hearts of men. Men respond to leadership in a most remarkable way and once you have won their hearts, they will follow you anywhere.

The price of success is hard work, dedication to the job at hand, and determination that whether we win or lose, we have applied the best of ourselves to the task at hand.

Individual commitment to a group effort is what makes a team work, a company work, a society work, a civilization work.

Heart power is the strength of any company. Heart power is the strength of the Green Bay Packers. Heart power is the strength of America.

Coaches who can outline plays on a blackboard are a dime a dozen. The ones who win get inside their players and motivate.

Lombardi's Rules for Success

- Develop mental toughness.
- Take the initiative.
- Stay in shape.
- Use time wisely.
- Make that second effort.

Good physical conditioning is essential to any occupation. A man who is physically fit performs better at any job. Fatigue makes cowards of us all.

Winning is not everything—but making the effort to win is.

The achievements of an organization are the results of the combined effort of each individual. After the cheers have died down and the stadium is empty, after the headlines have been written and after you are back in the quiet of your room, and the championship ring has been placed on the dresser and all the pomp and fanfare has faded, the enduring things that are left are: the dedication to excellence, the dedication to victory, and the dedication to doing with our lives the very best we can to make the world a better place in which to live.

I loved him because of his total absence of hypocrisy. I loved him because he was the best there ever was at what he did. I loved him because he had the curious capacity for making young men responsive to him without their feeling they had been abused.

–Howard Cosell, writer and broadcaster

What It Takes to Be Number One

Winning is not a sometime thing: it's an all-the-time thing. You don't win once in a while. You don't do things right once in a while. You do them right all the time. Winning is a habit. Unfortunately, so is losing.

Every time a football player goes out to ply his trade he's got to play from the ground up from the soles of his feet right up to his head. Every inch of him has to play. Some guys play with their heads, that's O.K. You've got to be smart to be No. 1 in any business, but more important, you've got to play with your heart, with every fiber of your body.

Running a football team is no different from running any other kind of organization, an army, a political party, a business. The principles are the same. The object is to win, to beat the other guy.

It's a reality of life that men are competitive and the most competitive games draw the most competitive men. They know the rules and the objectives when they get in the game. The objective is to win—fairly, squarely, by the rules, but to win.
In truth, I've never known a man worth his salt who in the long run, deep down in his heart, didn't appreciate the grind and the discipline. There is something in good men that really yearns for discipline and the harsh reality of head-to head combat.

Football is blocking and tackling. Everything else is mythology.

The harder you work, the harder it is to surrender.

Johnny Majors
Pittsburgh

Born: Lynchburg, Tenn.
College: Tennessee, 1957
Coached: Iowa State, Pittsburgh, Tennessee
Years: 29
Record: 185-137-10
Accomplishments:
- All-American tailback, 1956
- 16 bowl teams
- 1 national championship (Pittsburgh)
- 33-13-1 at Pitt
- 116-62-8 at Tennessee

No head coach can be better than his staff. Show me a winning team, and I'll show you a good group of assistant coaches.

❖

The first thing any coaching staff must do is weed out selfishness. No program can be successful with players who put themselves ahead of the team.

❖

It is my belief that discipline, well-earned pride, and a high degree of unselfishness contribute to achieving desirable morale...the most important element in building a successful team.

❖

Looking back over the years, the results of football training are most convincing. I know of no athletic competition that develops more useful traits of character or essential physical prowess. For example: the subordination of the individual to team play, development of initiative, leadership, and the value of persistence and physical fitness, the self-determination that inspires 'the will to win' against any odds—and along with it all, the building of real character and true sportsmanship.
> –Admiral Jones Ingram, Commander of Allied Forces in the South Atlantic, World War II

Wealth and status mean nothing on the football field;
effort and unselfishness mean everything.

A Man's Prayer
Grantland Rice

Let me live, oh Mighty Master, such a life as men shall know,
Tasting triumph and disaster, joy and not too much woe.
Let me run the gamut over, let me fight and love and laugh,
And when I'm beneath the clover let this be my epitaph.
Here lies one who took his chances in the busy world of men,
Battled luck and circumstances fought and fell and fought again.
Won sometimes but did no crowing, lost sometimes but did not wail,
Took his beating but kept going, never let his courage fail.
He was fallible and human, therefore loved and understood,
By both his fellow man and woman, whether good or not so good.
Kept his spirit undiminished, never laid down on a friend,
Played the game til it was finished, lived a sportsman till the end.

Profile of a Champion

Ambition: Has desire for high goals. Hates to lose. Cannot stand failure. Puts goals above ability.

Coachableness: Takes advice and is easy to coach. Eager to learn. Easy to approach. Follows rules and direction.

Aggression: A tiger! First-place-belongs-to-me type. Asserts himself.

Leadership: Shows the way and sets a good example. Respected by team members. Mixes well. Others follow his example and take his advice.

Take-Charge Guy: Takes over when things go wrong. Under pressure, he does something about the problem. Often a hero.

Hard Worker: One of the first to practice, the last to leave. Does extra hard work. Never misses practice. Follows instructions.

Physical Toughness: Develops toughness by hard work. In great condition. Keeps training rules and trains year-round.

Mental Toughness: Never gives in to his feelings. Has never-give-up attitude. Ignores heat, cold, pain.

Archie Manning
New Orleans Saints (Quarterback)

Born: Drew, Mississippi
College: Old Miss, 1971
Played: New Orleans Saints, Houston Oilers,
　　Minnesota Vikings
Accomplishments:
- Voted Mississippi's all-time greatest athlete
- 3rd in Heisman voting, 1970
- 1st-round draft pick, New Orleans
- NFC player of the year, 1974
- Sons Peyton and Eli now play in the NFL. Both were Heisman Trophy finalists (Peyton, second place; Eli, third place).

Football is the essence of America, but not because of championships or titles. The drive to compete, the guts to play, the will to come from behind, the grace to walk off the field a loser, that's the essence of football.

One guy can't do it by himself and it's a matter of recognizing this and giving others their share of the credit.

Bad teams are creative. They always find a new way to lose.

Deep inside, we're still the boys of autumn, the magic time of the year that once swept us on to America's football fields.

　　　　　　　　　　　　　　　–Manning, 10 years after his career was over

Build me a son, O Lord, who will be strong enough to know when he is weak, and brave enough to face himself when he is afraid, one who will be proud and unbending in honest defeat, and humble and gentle in victory.

　　　　　　　　　　　　　　　–General Douglas MacArthur

Charlie "Cholly Mac" McClendon
LSU

Born: Lewisville, AR
College: University of Kentucky
Coached: LSU
Years: 18
Record: 137-59-7
Accomplishments:
- 2 bowl teams as player for Bear Bryant
- Coached LSU's "Chinese Bandits" as assistant
- 1 conference championship
- 13 bowl games

Don't Quit
Author Unknown

When things go wrong, as they sometimes will,
When the road you're trudging seems all uphill,
When the funds are low and the debts are high,
And you want to smile but you have to sigh,
When care is pressing you down a bit—
Rest if you must but *don't you quit*.
Life is queer with its twists and turns,
As every one of us sometimes learns,
And many a fellow turns about,
Shen he might have won had he stuck it out.
Don't give up though the pace seems slow—
You may succeed with another blow.
Success is failure turned inside out—
The silver tint of the clouds of doubt,
You never can tell how close you are,
It may be near when it seems afar.
So stick to the fight when you're hardest hit—
It's when things seem worst, *you mustn't quit*.

We may have come in different ships, but we're all in the same boat now.

The worst mistake any coach can make is not being himself.

❖

In football, and in life, you've got to keep proving yourself.

❖

There is no single "best" way to do something in football.

❖

Courage to Succeed

Anonymous

If your desire can be called a wishbone, then your courage should be called your backbone. Your backbone gives you the gumption, the get-up-and-go, the guts to excel, the incentive to make any dream you dare to dream come true.

It's easy to be ordinary, but it takes courage to excel. It takes courage to sacrifice, to work out when you're tired or sick, to seek out tough competition when you know you'll probably get beat.

It takes courage to stand by your convictions when all those around you have no convictions.

It takes courage to keep fighting when you're losing.

It takes courage to stick to your game plan and the unrelenting pursuit of your goal when you encounter obstacles.

It takes courage to push yourself to places that you have never been before physically and mentally, to test your limits…to break through barriers.

It takes courage to run a marathon, but then how would you ever know how far you could run if you never tried?

I firmly believe we are put on earth to be tested, to be challenged with adversity and to see what we can accomplish. The successful person is the one who continually faces problems and challenges, and overcomes them—the person who has the courage to keep going no matter how many obstacles stand in the way—the person who has the courage to look deep into his own soul.

Sebastian Coe used the word courage to describe what it will take to run the super mile. He didn't say mental toughness, which is what you need at the end when your legs are dead and your lungs are bursting. Most good athletes can handle this; they can fight through the pain barrier. What Coe is saying is that you must be courageous, you must be brave enough to push yourself at the beginning when you're not hurting, knowing full well that the more you push yourself at the beginning, the more you'll hurt at the end. This is courage.

John McKay
Southern Cal

Born: Everettsville, West Virginia
College: Purdue, University of Oregon,1950
Coached: Southern Cal, Tampa Bay Buccaneers
Years: 25
Record: 171-128-9
Accomplishments:
- 4 national championships
- 127-40-8 (.749) in 16 years as Southern Cal
- 9 conference championships
- 3 undefeated seasons
- 5 Rose Bowl victories
- 40 First-Team All-Americans
- 44-88-1 with Tampa Bay

Losing is always harder on the coach than the players. The players lose a game and they still go to a dance afterwards. For the coaches there is no dancing.

There are still over one billion Chinese who don't care if we win or lose.

If going to bed early the night before a game helps you win, why don't we put them in bed at 3:00 in the afternoon?

Hold at home. Don't hold on the road.
—McKay, on referees calling holding

The only problem with doing the impossible is that everyone wants you to do it again next week.

We didn't tackle well today, but we made up for it by not blocking.
—McKay, after a loss

McKay, in the locker room after a 3-0 loss to Oregon State: If anyone needs to take a shower, hurry up and do so!

I am a big believer in the "Mirror Test." All that matters is if you can look in the mirror and honestly tell the person you see there that you've done your very best.

The players yell a lot in practice. We probably rank in the top 3 yelling teams in the nation. Yelling doesn't do a damn thing on Saturday.

On praying in the locker room: God's busy. They'll have to make do with me.

If you have everyone back from a team that went 1-10, how important is experience?

A genius in coaching is a guy who won last week.

A runner must understand that there's one bad thing about carrying that football—it attracts a crowd.

When you scrape away all the hayseed, you find you're looking at the royal flush underneath. You can beat the Bear once. But never the same way twice.
—McKay, on friend Bear Bryant

McKay, when asked by a reporter about his Tampa Bay team's execution after a close loss: I think it's a good idea!

Underdog, overdog, hotdog. What you want to be is the underdog with the best team.

What Is the Price of Success for a Coach?
Author Unknown

To use all of your courage to force yourself to concentrate on the problem at hand, to think of it deeply and constantly, to study it from all angles.

To have a high and sustained determination to put over what you plan to accomplish, not if circumstance be favorable to its accomplishment, but in spite of all adverse circumstances which may arise. Nothing worthwhile has ever been accomplished without some obstacles to overcome.

So refuse to believe that there are any circumstances sufficiently strong to defeat you in the accomplishment of your purpose, victory.

What to Look for in an Athlete
McKay at Southern Cal

- Spirit of competition! Being persistent. Never take no for an answer when there is a job to do, a pass to be caught, speed to get up, etc. I remember backs or linemen of the past by their techniques, as much as by their fire and combative spirit.
- Coachability! Can he take coaching? Can he take criticism and not always be looking for an alibi? Is he a "know-it-all"? Or does he do his level best to try to improve?
- Willingness to practice. Does he want to improve? Is he willing to put in the long, grinding hours that are necessary? Is he the first guy out with a smile on his face, or the last one out with a frown?
- Willingness to make the necessary sacrifices. This means conditioning and conditioning is not fun. It is punishment in every sense of the word.
- Ability to think under fire. Can he shut out from his mind everything except the work to be done at the moment? This does not take a great brain but it takes concentration.
- Willingness and ability to shut out all personal feeling about the opponent, except to hit him as hard and as quick as you can in a *fair way* with everything you've got. It never pays to get personal. Do your job.
- Ability. Muscular coordination. We don't all have it to the same extent, but we can make up for the lack of it in some of the above-mentioned items.
- Speed. The ability to move fast or quick. There is a difference and they can both be developed by hard work and concentration.

"Broadway" Joe Namath
New York Jets (Quarterback)

Born: Beaver Falls, PA
College: Alabama 1964
Played: New York Jets, Los Angeles Rams
Accomplishments:
- Super Bowl III champion, 1969
- Super Bowl MVP, AFL MVP, Pro Player of the Year, 1968
- 6 pro baseball teams offered him contracts in high school
- 10-1 record as a sophomore at Alabama
- Cotton Bowl MVP, 1964

If you aren't going all the way, why go at all?

The Jets will beat the Colts, I guarantee it.
> —Namath, before Super Bowl III, despite the Jets being 17- to 24-point underdogs. Final score: Jets 16, Colts 7.

If you want to be first-class, you've got to act first-class.

❖

Nobody wants to follow somebody who doesn't know where he's going.

When you have confidence, you can have a lot of fun, and when you're having fun, you can do amazing things.
> —Author unknown

Dear Lord,
In this battle that goes on through life,
I ask but a field that is fair.
A chance to compete with all in the strife,
And courage to strive and dare.
And if I should win, let it be by this code
With my faith and my honor held high.
And if I should lose, let me stand by the road,
And cheer as the winner goes by

Pride
Anonymous

It's easy to quit without pride. Pride is something that has to be developed. The better person you are, the harder you work, the greater your sacrifice, the more pride you will have.

Are you proud of yourself? If not, why not? Eliminate the negative elements of your life and push towards the positive, toward a goal. Strive to become the best person, the best student, the best athlete that you can become.

You won't gain any pride by a half-hearted performance. The level of your pride is, therefore, directly proportional to the extent of your effort.

There never was a great athlete who was a good loser. A good sport, yes, but not a good loser. Good losers lose often; maybe that's why they're good at it.

When two athletes have:
    Equal natural ability,
    Equal preparation,
    Equal conditioning,
    Equal concentration,
    Equal reaction to pressure,
    Who will have the edge? Who will win?

The answer is simple—the athlete with competitive greatness—the athlete who is at his very best when his very best is needed—the athlete who loves a hard battle—the athlete who refuses to lose—the athlete who has the most pride. No matter what happens to you—never let them take away your pride.

General Robert Neyland
Tennessee

Born: Greenville, Texas
College: West Point
Coached: Tennessee
Years: 21
Record: 173-31-12
Accomplishments:
- 6 bowl games
- 3 national championships
- 1939 team held every opponent scoreless
- 1938–1939 teams went 71 consecutive quarters without being scored on

Look to the day—for it is life—the very life of life. In its brief counsel lie all the verities and realities of your existence! The bliss of growth, the glory of action, the splendor of beauty. For yesterday is already a dream and tomorrow is only a vision, but today, well lived, makes every yesterday a dream of happiness and every tomorrow a vision of hope. Look well, therefore, to this day. Such is the salutation of the dawn.

–The Sanskrit

A football team is like an army. Your men must be in good physical condition. They must have technical ability, and they must have high morale.

Football is nothing more than a series of mistakes, actions, and miscalculations. Punt and let your opponent make them.

The first thing any coaching staff must do is weed out selfishness. No program can be successful with players who put themselves ahead of the team.

To be good, a team must have good seniors.

Are you a part of our problem or a part of our solution?

To defeat a weak opponent is not the objective.
The objective is to win when he is as good or better than you.

Football is a game of defense and field position. You can score three ways on offense and four ways on defense.

In the struggle between equal teams, the difference is never physical but invariably mental.

The teams that make the fewest mistakes usually win.

The cornerstone to victory is self-faith, resolution, and confidence in ultimate success.

One reason most of us don't get what we want out of life is because we don't *know* what we want. We settle for whatever comes along. We never clearly define our objective, even to ourselves. Is it any wonder that the wishful arrows we shoot in the general direction of the target seldom hit it?

It may sound ridiculous to some, but there is considerable evidence to prove that people can be pretty much what they *want* to—if they will decide what that is and concentrate *all* their thoughts and actions toward it. A person's powers—often unrealized—have a way of matching his dreams. You can't win, however, just wishing. You must concentrate everything you have on reaching your goal—and give up everything that stands in the way.

It takes a lot out of you to bear down as hard as you must, but it can be done.

Tom Osborne
Nebraska

Born: Hastings, Nebraska
College: Hastings
Coached: Nebraska
Years: 25
Record: 255-49-3
Accomplishments:
- 3 national championships
- 25 straight bowl games
- Never less than 9 wins in a season; averaged 10 wins a season
- Winningest coach in Big Eight history
- 11 league championships
- Elected to U.S. Congress (Nebraska), 2000

With the right preparation anything is possible.

❖

I celebrate a victory when I start walking off the field.
By the time I reach the locker room, I'm done.

❖

If your only mission is to win football games, you'll never win enough to find fulfillment.

❖

I learned from Warren Buffett. I look for three things, intelligence, energy, and character. If they don't have the last one the first two will kill you.

–Osborne, on hiring

❖

I try to live one day at a time, and not worry about tomorrow. I try to live a disciplined life and accept the result of that disciplined life as the will of God.

❖

Everyone is a role model to someone and your impact might not be known for 25 or 30 years.

Victory is achieved before, not during, the game.

Balance your life, intellectual and spiritual. You can't be one dimensional and be happy.

Many of the things we pursue, such as popularity, money, and public approval, are very transitory. In the final analysis, the only enduring factor that we have to show for our stay on Earth is the quality of our character.

Witness always, use words when necessary.

Ultimately, the effect you leave on the people around you is the legacy you leave.

Sign in the Nebraska Football Locker Room
Coach Osborne

Even though we have been good in other years, this year holds no guarantee. Success doesn't come automatically. Fans are fans. Some will stick with you, some won't. The only people who really understand, the ones you can count on beyond a doubt, who will be with you whether you are 8-and-3 or 3-and-8, are the people in *this room*.

Bill Parcells
Dallas Cowboys

Active

Born: Englewood, New Jersey
College: Colgate
Coached: New York Giants, New England Patriots, New York Jets, Dallas Cowboys
Years: 16
Record: 159–112-1
Accomplishments:
- Won 2 Super Bowls with the Giants
- Took the Patriots to the 1997 Super Bowl
- The only coach in NFL history to lead 3 different franchises to Conference Championship games

The best coach I've ever seen on game day.
>   —Tom Boisture, New York Giants front office, on Parcells

If I was as good a coach as that man, I'd coach football forever.
>   —Maurice Carthon, Jets running back coach, on Parcells

Parking lot players—the kind of guy who just nods his head, packs his bag, and shows up early if I told him we were playing in a parking lot, for no money, at 6 AM Wednesday morning.

Coaching is about human interaction and trying to know your players.

I would like my legacy to be that my players thought I tried as hard as I could to win every game.

Train your team for strength, stamina, and endurance and you'll have good results.

Winning doesn't feel as good as it used to and losing feels worse…This is my crack cocaine. I know it's like an assembly line. I know that some day the line is going to stop, and that's when you're Just Another Guy.

Dumb players do dumb things. Smart players seldom do dumb things.

If he tells you there's cheese on top of the mountain, you'd better bring crackers.
—Keith Byars, Jets running back, on Parcells

If he told his players the Earth were flat, none of them would cross the street. He could stare at a blue sky so hard, it becomes cloudy.
—Phil Simms, New York Giants quarterback

A punt return for a touchdown or a substantial field-position gain equates to the same kind of game that a 100-yard rusher would produce—you win 70 percent of those games.

What I look for in a coach: Someone who is consistent, who is not afraid to confront the players, who makes the players accountable for their performance, will not take excuses and is a very good teacher.

❖

You never want to go into a game with a tired team.

❖

Coaches have to accept the fact that football isn't for everyone.

❖

I have always felt, based on rough statistical analysis I did a long time ago, that 100 yards of field position created would generally equate to six or seven points. But the way to understand 100 yards is not just in total offense or total defense statistics. It's also in the return game and in turnovers.

Turnovers are especially important because of field position changes. Turnovers are the most significant statistic when it comes to winning and losing in football. A turnover is really 40 yards in field position. When you turn the ball over, you lose the opportunity to punt.

❖

Teams that can create a yardage advantage in areas like fewer penalties win games.

❖

Coaches sometime fall into the trap of giving young players too much too soon. He can't have too many things to think about

❖

When you want to get players attention—you scrimmage.

❖

If wind is a factor, be conservative going into it, open up going with it. Have a plan for wind management.

❖

If you're sensitive, you will have a hard time with me.

❖

If you respect a player and he respects you, then you have a relationship, and in a relationship all commentary is allowed.

❖

Rule: Never complain about officiating. It does no good. During the game I don't want to be fighting two opponents.

❖

Whatever I give as a coach, I took as a player.

❖

If you can hold a team to 17 points you ought to win.

The only players I hurt with my words are the ones who have an inflated opinion of their ability.

The ability I have as a coach is to see the end picture. I know what it takes to get a team to reach its full potential, and I want players who want to reach their full potential.

From the Camp of the Beaten
Grantland Rice

I have learned something well worth while,
That victory could not bring
To wipe the blood from my mouth and smile,
Where none can see the string.
I can walk head up, while my heart is down,
From the beating that brought its good,
And that means more than the champion's crown,
Who is taking the easier road.

I have learned something worth far more,
Than victory brings to men;
Battered and beaten, bruised and sore,
I can still come back again.
Crowded back in the hard, tough race,
I've found that I have the heart,
To look raw failure in the face,
And train for another start.

Winners who wear the victor's wreath,
Looking for softer ways,
Watch for my blade as it leaves the sheath,
Sharpened on rougher days,
Trained upon pain and punishment,
I've groped my way through the night,
But the flag still flies from my battle tent,
And I've only begun to fight…

More than other athletes football players want to be led and Bill Parcels leads.
                                    –Phil Simms, New York Giants quarterback

As a coach I prepare myself to bring high energy to every practice and every meeting.

❖

Our stature as a nation depends fundamentally on the strength and character of our people, not on our MBA programs, trade policies, business acumen, or number of engineers, important though they are.

–Gerald Ford, 38th President of the United States,
and former center at the University of Michigan

❖

Discipline–Organization–Consistency
Locker Room Wall

Every winning team has a game plan. So does the winning athlete. You have a goal; now, sit down and figure out a training schedule that will let you reach that goal.

Organize a practice schedule.

Have the discipline to follow it. Be consistent in your workouts. Have a no-nonsense attitude at practice; work hard, and you'll improve every day. Come early and stay late, not for your coaches or your teammates, but for yourself. Improving yourself is the best way to help your team.

During the off-season, write down how many hours you want to work out each day. If you are consistent, you'll work out every day, rain or shine. You'll do it not for a month, but month after month, pushing yourself after the initial excitement wears off.

How many people do you know who were going to dedicate themselves to a sport, who lifted weights enthusiastically for the first month, but then decided it would be ok to miss just one workout? Missing the first workout is like telling a lie—the next one comes easier. And, you will never be able to make up the day you missed.

I don't agree with the people who say that you must spend every minute of every day working toward your goal. If you did this, you would flunk out of school, alienate your family, and have no friends. This is why you need a schedule—a game plan—and it's your discipline that will keep you on your schedule. This schedule should also include time for your family, your schoolwork, and your friends. If it calls for a two-hour workout every day, make sure you put in two hard, intense, concentrated hours—follow your game plan. When you are finished, mark off another day for yourself. Then, you can work on your studies, go to a concert, or whatever—you'll not only have a great time, but you'll also feel good about yourself.

Along the way, you should develop tunnel vision. Set your sight on a goal; then don't take your eyes off it until you reach that goal. Put on your blinders—you'll need them today because our world is filled with so many good things to do, so many fun things, that you'll easily get distracted. Today, you not only have to choose between the good and the bad—you have to choose between the good and the good.

Joe Paterno
Penn State

Active

Born: Brooklyn, New York
College: Brown, 1951
Coached: Penn State
Years: 38
Record: 339-109-3
Accomplishments:
- 30 bowl games (20-9-1); has won every major bowl game at least once
- 2 national championships
- 5 undefeated, untied seasons

It isn't the plays or the system that gets the job done, it's the quality of the people in the system.

❖

You have to perform at a consistently higher level than others. That's the mark of a true professional.

❖

Macho does not prove mucho.

❖

Act like you expect to get into the end zone.

❖

Bite off more than you can chew,
Then chew it.
Plan more than you can do,
Then do it.

❖

Keep hustling, every day, every play. No matter how bad things look, something good is going to happen.

If I ever need a brain transplant, I want one from a sportswriter, I'll know it's never been used.

❖

Publicity is like poison. It doesn't hurt unless you swallow it.

❖

If we win the national championship, so what? It sounds corn-ball, but that's the way I feel. My best team will be the one that produces the best doctors, lawyers, fathers, and citizens, not necessarily the one with the best record. Let's keep football in context.

❖

Failure is not the worst thing in the world. The very worst thing is not to try.

❖

You Decide
Author Unknown

Each player must decide,
Whether he will do it or toss it aside.
You are the fellow who makes up your mind,
Whether you'll lead or linger behind.
Whether you'll try for the goal that's afar,
Or be contented to stay where you are.
Take it or leave it. Here's something to do,
Just think it over. It's all up to you!
Scorned for a loner or praised by your chief,
Rich man or poor man, beggar or thief?
Eager or earnest or dull through the day,
Honest or crooked it's you who must say!
You must decide in the face of the test,
Whether you'll shirk it or give it your best.

Ten Characteristics of a Good Coach
Bron Bacevich, Roger Bacon High School, Cincinnati

- Persistence. A strong coach hangs on a little longer, works a little harder.
- Imagination. He harnesses imagination to practical plans that produce results.
- Vision. The present is just the beginning. A good coach is impressed with the possibilities of the future.
- Sincerity. A good coach can be trusted.
- Integrity. A good coach has principles and lives by them.
- Poise. A good coach isn't overbearing, but is friendly, and assured.
- Thoughtfulness. He is considerate, aware.
- Common Sense. A good coach has common sense, which is not all that common.
- Altruism. A good coach lives by the Golden Rule.
- Initiative. He gets things started now and he gets things done, no matter how long it takes.

13 Rules to Live By
Colin Powell

1. It ain't as bad as you think. It will look better in the morning.
2. Get mad; then get over it.
3. Avoid having your ego so close to your position that, when your position fails, your ego goes with it.
4. It can be done!
5. Be careful what you choose. You may get it.
6. Don't let adverse facts stand in the way of a good decision.
7. You can't make someone else's choices. You shouldn't let someone else make yours.
8. Check small things.
9. Share credit.
10. Remain calm. Be kind.
11. Have a vision. Be demanding.
12. Don't take counsel of your fears or naysayers.
13. Perpetual optimism is a force multiplier.

George Perles
Michigan State

Born: Detroit, Michigan
College: Michigan State, 1960
Coached: Michigan State, Pittsburgh Steelers (assistant)
Years: 11
Record: 72-61-4
Accomplishments:
- 7 bowl games
- 2 Big Ten championships
- 1 Michigan High School Championship with St. Ambrose High School
- 4 Steelers Super Bowl wins with Perles as defensive coordinator

Your family and God first, then your education, and last football.

❖

You're one injury away from playing your last game.

❖

If you forgot your assignment forget it full speed. Hit someone.

❖

Great players make great plays in games that count.

❖

Prepare and practice for each game as if it were the only game you were going to play that season: ND, Michigan or Northwestern, Indiana... They all count one!

❖

You ask me a question, you'll get an answer. You might not like what you hear, but you'll get what I think is an honest answer.

❖

Work hard, keep your mouth shut, and good things will happen.

The 24 Hour Rule: Win or lose, celebrate or mourn for 24 hours, then get back to work.

All bowl games are great, like eating ham, and I never had a bad piece of ham.

I want my players to be mean tough son of a guns on the field and perfect gentlemen off the field.

The Desirable Traits of a Military Leader

Bearing: Creating a favorable impression in carriage appearance, and personal conduct at all times.

Courage (Physical and Moral): A mental quality which recognizes fear of danger or criticism but enables the individual to meet danger or opposition with calmness and firmness.

Decisiveness: Ability to make decisions promptly and then express them in a clear and forceful manner.

Dependability: The certainty of proper performance of duty with loyalty to seniors and subordinates.

Endurance: Mental and physical stamina measured by the ability to stand pain, fatigue, distress, and hardship.

Enthusiasm: The display of sincere interest and exuberance in the performance of duties.

Initiative: A quality of seeing what has to be done and commencing a course of action.

Integrity: Uprightness of character and soundness of moral principle: the quality of absolute truthfulness and honesty.

Judgment: Weighing facts and possible solutions on which to base a sound decision.

Justice: Being impartial and consistent in exercising command.

Knowledge: Acquired information including professional knowledge and an understanding of your subordinates.

Loyalty: Faithfulness to country, the Army, your unit, your seniors, and subordinates.

Tact: The ability to deal with others without creating offense.

Unselfishness: The avoidance of providing for one's own comfort and personal advancement at the expense of others.

Coach's Prayer of Thanks
Author Unknown

Dear God, thank you for the opportunities and challenges you have blessed us with. Help us to love our moms and dads, our families, our friends, relatives, and teammates as You love us.

Help us to sacrifice our personal welfare for others as You did for us, and help us to utilize our athletic abilities to glorify Your name.

For it is only in giving that we emulate You. I pray that we may always be true sportsman on the gridiron of life.

May we learn to obey life's rules so that we may be spared its harsh penalties. Learn to prize honest defeat above a dishonest victory. Be brave in defeat, humble in victory.

When we strive to become a better athlete, may these conversion attempts succeed. May we so play the game that someday the Divine Referee will include us in His Hall of Fame.
Amen.

A Football Coach Prays
Author Unknown

I suppose I should ask for flashy backs,
Whose hips are on a swivel.
And whose speed make people say,
"Boy, they run to beat the devil."
I ought to include a massive line,
With chassis like Mack trucks,
Whose strength scares all opponents,
And drops them like sitting ducks.
I could ask for a team with precision,
Whose efforts would honors take,
And also plead for a squad with brains,
Who never make a mistake.
But Lord, I am an understandable coach,
The talent cannot be all mine,
So if you give me the things I want,
I'll never complain or whine.
Just give me a bunch of eager boys,
With the spirit to fight and win,
Who will battle as soon as they take the field,
And most of all never give in!

Eddie Robinson
Grambling

Born: Jackson, Louisiana
College: Leland, 1941
Coached: Grambling
Years: 56
Record: 408-165-15
Accomplishments:

- Winningest college football coach of all time
- 9 Black National College Championships
- 17 Southwest Athletic Conference Championships
- 43 Grambling players in pro camps in 1971
- 1966, voted the coach who had the biggest impact on college football
- Over 200 Grambling players played in the NFL

I don't believe anybody can out-American me. I know I sometimes sound like a politician at a Fourth of July picnic, but I feel I am telling the truth when I tell people that we live in the greatest country in the world.

The real records I have set over 56 years are the fact that I have had one job and one wife.

I'm not concerned about personal records. Time takes care of everything and it will eventually take care of that. All it means is that I've been around a long time.
                    —Robinson, on breaking Paul (Bear) Bryant's all-time wins record

I haven't blocked or tackled anybody. I have just tried to give encouragement to the young men who have played for Grambling. The record belongs to everybody, all the former players, all the assistant coaches, and all the loyal fans that have supported Grambling throughout the years. Eddie Robinson sure hasn't done it alone.

Coach a boy as if he were your own son.

I've seen that glint in Eddie Robinson's eye. He's got that old look you get when you're about to kill a gnat with a sledgehammer.

–An opponent, just before playing Grambling

Win without braggin'. Lose without acting like a foul.

Leadership, like coaching, is fighting for the hearts and souls of your men and getting them to believe in you.

You can have anything you want if you're willing to pay the price.

I always blame Eddie Robinson. I try to figure out where I've failed. I don't ever tear the ball club down. We don't make excuses. Sometimes we just get whipped.

–Robinson, on losing

My players can wear their hair as long as they want and dress any way that they want. That is, if they are paying their own tuition, room, and board.

Every man on the team has a right to play… some more than others.

Knute Rockne
Notre Dame

Born: Voss, Norway
College: Notre Dame, 1913
Coached: Notre Dame
Years: 13
Record: 105-12-5
Accomplishments:
- 5 undefeated seasons
- 1 bowl game
- Highest winning percentage ever in college football (.881)
- 3 national championships

Be more concerned with your character than with your reputation, because your character is what you really are, while your reputation is merely what others think you are.

Rockne, poking his head inside the door of the locker room after his team had been mauled in the first half of a game: Oh, excuse me, ladies! I thought this was the Notre Dame locker room.

The real secret to winning football games is to work more as a team, and think team first and less about the individual. I play not my eleven best but my best eleven that think as one.

Football is mostly played from the neck up.

I've found that plays work best when you have big players.

You can only coast one way, whether it be in sports or business, and that's downhill.

Rockne, when asked after a game why Notre Dame had lost: I won't know until my barber tells me on Monday.

An automobile goes nowhere efficiently unless it has a quick, hot spark to ignite things, to set the cogs of the machine in motion. So I try to make every player on my team feel he's the spark keeping our machine in motion. On him depends our success.

Courage means being afraid to do something, but still doing it.

Leaders are like eagles. . .they don't flock. You find them flying alone.

What Are You Doing Now
R. Rhodes Stabley

It matters not if you lost the fight,
And were badly beaten too.
It matters not if you failed outright,
In the things you tried to do.
It matters not if you toppled down,
From the azure heights of blue,
But what are you doing now????

It matters not if your plans were foiled,
And your hopes have fallen through.
It matters not if your chance was spoiled,
With the gain almost in view.
It matters not if you missed the goal,
though you struggled brave and true,
But what are you doing now????

It matters not if your fortune's gone,
And your fame has vanished too.
It matters not if a cruel world's scorn,
Be directed straight at you.
It matters not if the worst has come,
And your dreams have not come true,
But what are you doing now????

Courage is the first of human qualities because it is the quality which guarantees all others.
–Winston Churchill, Prime Minister of Great Britain during WWII

Success is never final and failure is never fatal. It is courage that counts.

Never, never, never, never give up!

Leadership

Loyalty: Probably the most important word of all, arising out of integrity. No person has ever achieved leadership without loyalty to the cause, to the job, to colleagues, to superiors, and to subordinates.

Enthusiasm: For life; for the task; for people; for little and big things; for achievement.

Attitude: A leader has a healthy attitude toward the task at hand. Conceit and leadership are incompatible with each other. Be humble.

Dedication: Of person, service, and effort to accomplish.

Example: One leads by what he is and what he does.

Responsibility: A working word! A leader is always ready to accept responsibility.

Scholarship: No leader has ever survived without showing a desire to improve his skills and capacity to study, to learn, to think.

Humor: A leader must have a sense of humor to evaluate properly both the serious and the lighter sides of life.

Initiative: A leader must know how and when to step in and do a job without being told or directed, and see the task through to its conclusion.

Personality: All leaders develop a significant personality. This does not necessarily mean extrovert or "outgoing," but a personality that embraces honesty, fairness, understanding, and, above all, high moral standards.

The Legend of the Four Horsemen of Notre Dame
Grantland Rice

Outlined against a blue-gray October sky, the Four Horsemen rode again. In dramatic lore they are known as Famine, Pestilence, Destruction, and Death. These are only aliases. Their real names are Stuhldreher, Miller, Crowley, and Layden.
–Written in the *New York Herald-Tribune* on
October 19, 1924, to describe the Notre Dame backfield

Darrell Royal
Texas

Born: Hollis, Oklahoma
College: Oklahoma, 1950
Coached: Mississippi State, Washington, Texas
Years: 23
Record: 184-60-5
Accomplishments:
- Never had a losing season
- 3 national championships
- 11 Southwest Conference championships (including 6 consecutive)
- 16 bowl games

Only angry people win football games.

❖

The only way I know to keep football fun is to win. There is no laughter in losing.

❖

Luck is what happens when preparation meets opportunity.

❖

When it gets right down to the wood-chopping, the key to winning is confidence.

❖

The real make of a man is how he treats people who can never do anything for him.

❖

On game day, I'm as nervous as a pig visiting a packing plant.

❖

Never try to fool a player. You can't ever kid a kid.

You've got to work yourself into a position for luck to happen. Luck doesn't go around looking for a stumblebum.

❖

Too many players think they can push themselves forward by patting themselves on the back.

❖

You can't be aggressive and confused at the same time.

❖

A coach isn't as smart as they say he is when he wins, or as stupid when he loses.

❖

The Big Game
Author Unknown

You take the color and the flash of the game,
The roar of the crowds, with their breasts aflame,
And all the pageant that waits the call,
As the toe drives into the waiting ball.
But leave me the halfback's driving might,
The surging lines in a bitter fight,
The sweat and smear for the warring soul,
As the tackle opens a two-foot hole.
The human gardens of rose-lip girls,
The ringing cheers, with there eddying swirls,
The interference, the deadly pass,
The grip and crash of the swirling mass.
For the crowd fades out and the cheers dip low,
When the fourth down comes, with a yard to go,
And the knightly tourneys that used to be,
In the golden era of chivalry.
The world grows soft as the years advance,
Further and further from sword and lance,
When the cavemen, after his morning's fun,
Slew the mammoth and mastodon.
But his ghost at the gridiron calls through space;
"These, too, are worthy to build a race."

I don't want any candy stripes on our uniforms.
I teach our players these are work clothes.

A head coach is guided by this main objective: dig, claw, wheedle, coax that fanatical effort out of the players. You want them to play every Saturday as if they were planting the flag on Iwo Jima.

Fat people don't offend me. What offends me is losing with fat people.

The most important ingredient in your locker is your attitude.

Football doesn't build character. It eliminates those without it.

Ten Commandments of Success
Charles Schwab

1. Work hard. Hard work is the best investment a man can make.
2. Study hard. Knowledge enables a man to work more intelligently and effectively.
3. Have initiative. Ruts often deepen into graves.
4. Love your work. Then you will find pleasure in mastering it.
5. Be exact. Slipshod methods bring only slipshod results.
6. Have the American spirit of conquest. Thus you can successfully battle with and overcome difficulty.
7. Cultivate personality. Personality is to a man what perfume is to a flower.
8. Help and share with others. The real test of business greatness lies in giving opportunity to others.
9. Be democratic. Unless you feel right towards your fellow man, you can never be a successful leader of men.
10. In all things do your best. The man who has done his best, has done everything. The man who has done less than his best has done nothing.

Glen "Bo" Schembechler
Michigan

Born: Barberton, Ohio
College: Miami of Ohio
Coached: Miami of Ohio, Michigan
Years: 27
Record: 234-65-8
Accomplishments:
- Never had a losing season
- 17 bowl games
- 13 Big Ten championships in 21 seasons at Michigan
- 2 Mid American championships in 6 seasons at Miami of Ohio

The reason some men do not succeed is because their wishbone is where their backbone ought to be.

Leaders must coach and teach attitude every day.

I tell my people: you treat me fair, I'll treat you fair. You tell me the truth. I'll tell you the truth. You may hate my guts because you believe something I don't, but we'll both know where we stand.

My biggest problems are defensive linemen and offensive alumni.

You want to win? Just do the work that has to be done. The dirty every day, down-in-the-trenches work, and do it with enthusiasm.

When your team is winning, be ready to be tough, because winning can make you soft. On the other hand, when your team is losing stick by them. Keep believing.

Any fool can criticize condemn, complain—and most fools do!

Every individual in your organization must know exactly the team's goals and must set individual goals to achieve them.

Football's Answer

Unknown Coach, 1920

They reform me each new season,
As they point to each new fault.
And their hands are turned against me,
As they crowd me to the vault.
But amid the growing clamor,
They still know around the clan,
I'm the soul of college spirit,
And the maker of a man.

Oh, I know I'm far from perfect,
When the autumn leaves turn red,
When the tackle's neck is furrowed,
By the halfback's heavy tread:
But you hear them still admitting,
As they put me on the pan,
"He's the soul of college spirit,
And the maker of a man."

Perhaps I'm over featured,
In the headline's stirring plea.
Perhaps I'm more important,
Than a mere game ought to be.
But with all the sins they speak of,
And the list is quite a span,
I'm the soul of college spirit,
And the maker of a man.

No coach in America asks any man to make any sacrifice. He requests that he do the opposite—live clean, come clean, think clean—and stop doing all the things that destroy him mentally, morally, and physically and start doing the things that will make him a man.
—Fielding "Hurry Up" Yost, the legendary coach of the Michigan Wolverines in the early 1900s and winner of the first Rose Bowl (1901)

Don Shula
Miami Dolphins

Born: Painesville, Ohio
College: John Carroll, Ohio
Coached: Baltimore Colts, Miami Dolphins
Years: 33
Record: 347-173-6
Accomplishments:
- Most victories in NFL history
- NFL Hall of Fame, 1997
- 2 Super Bowl championships
- 6 Super Bowl teams
- Only NFL coach to go undefeated in a season (1972, 17-0)
- Shula's teams were always among the least-penalized in the NFL

The superior man blames himself—the inferior man blames another.

Winning is not final.

I tried every game to be the best I could and make my team the best it could be.

Coaches have a tendency to stay too long with people with potential. Try to avoid those players and go with a proven attitude. Players who live on potential are coach killers. As soon as you find out who the coach killers are on your team, the better off you are. Go with the guys who have less talent but more dedication, more singleness of purpose.

Have the best people on the field in critical situations.

You win with good people. Character is just as important as ability.

Coaches Never Lose
Unknown Coach

A team can lose. Any team can lose. But in a very real sense, a coach never loses. For a coach has two tasks. The minor one is to teach skills; how to run faster, hit harder, block better, kick farther, and jump higher.

The second task—the major task—is to make men out of boys. It's to teach them to be humble in victory and proud in defeat. This goes without saying. But more importantly, it's to teach them to live up to their potential no matter what that potential is. It's to teach them to do their best and never be satisfied with what they are but to strive to be as good as they can be if they tried harder.

A coach can never make a great player out of a boy who isn't potentially great. But he can make a competitor out of any kid, and miraculously he can make a man out of a boy.

For a coach the final score doesn't read so many points for my team, so many points for theirs. Instead it reads: so many men out of so many boys, this is a score that is never published. This is the score that he reads to himself and in which he finds his real joy when the games are long over and he has blown his last whistle

Just a Little More
Unknown Coach

The thing that makes a champion is obvious enough:
It isn't any mystic prestidigitator's stuff.
It's nothing more than giving to whatever be the chore,
The power is within you—and a small scintilla more.
It isn't any wizardry, it's not a magic gift,
It's merely lifting honestly the load you have to lift,
Or, in the game you're playing, it is using all your store,
Of grit and nerve and energy—and just a trifle more.
The thing that makes a champion is simple, plain, and clear,
It's never being "almost," "just about," or "pretty near."
It's summoning the utmost from your spirit's inner core,
And giving every bit of it—and just a little bit more.
"That little more—how much it is."
As deep and wide and far,
As the enormous emptiness from a molehill to a star,
The gulf between the earthbound and the eagles as they soar,
The champions give their best—and one iota more.

The Winning Edge

The words "winning edge" represent a concept for achieving victory that I brought with me to Miami. They are linked together, much as a ring links man and woman together in marriage.

You set a goal to be the best and then you work every waking hour of each day trying to achieve that goal.

The ultimate goal is victory, and if you refuse to work as hard as you possibly can toward that aim, or if you do anything that keeps you from achieving that goal, you are just cheating yourself. I feel that way about athletics, but more importantly, I feel that way about life in general.

Extra study, extra determination, extra gassers, and extra effort cover three areas that I feel are keys to success—mental, physical, and emotional.

We want the Dolphins to be better prepared mentally than our opponents and realize the importance of not making mental errors in a game. A player can be the greatest physical specimen and execute flawlessly in practice, but if he can't carry out the detail of his assignment in a stress situation during a game on Sunday afternoon, he really isn't of significant value.

All things being equal, the team that has the best-conditioned athletes and the fastest ones will have the winning edge. I am a stickler on condition.

I demand total involvement from our players. After God and family, the only other thing that's important is what the Dolphins do on game day.

What we want to dedicate ourselves to is establishing a standard of excellence in the future and we are always looking for "the winning edge."

Learn from everyone, copy no one.

Sure, luck means a lot in football. Not having a good quarterback is bad luck.

My coaching philosophy? Determine your players' talents and then give them every weapon to get the most from those talents.

Never take your focus away from the next game.
Lots of leaders want to be popular. I never cared about that. I want to be respected.

Ken "Snake" Stabler
Oakland Raiders (Quarterback)

Born: Foley, Alabama
College: Alabama
Played: Oakland Raiders (10 years)
Accomplishments:
- Super Bowl Champions, 1977
- All-American
- 5-time All-Pro
- Passed for more than 200 yards 36 times
- 3 SEC championships
- 2 national championships
- 0 interceptions in 145 attempts (Oakland)

Four Characteristics Usually Found in Highly Successful Coaches

Consistency. These folk are not restless flashes in the pan, here today, gone tomorrow. Neither are they given to fads and gimmicks. Those who impact lives stay at the task with reliable regularity. They seem unaffected by the fickle winds of change. They're consistent.

Authenticity. Probe all you wish, try all you like to find hypocrisy, and you search in vain. People who impact others are real to the core—no alloy covered over with a brittle layer of chrome—but solid, genuine stuff right down to the nubbies. They're authentic.

Unselfishness. Mustn't forget this one! Hands down, it's there every time. Those who impact us the most watch out for themselves the least. They notice our needs and reach out to help, honestly concerned about our welfare. Their least-used words are "I," "me," "my," and "mine." They're unselfish.

Tirelessness. With relentless determination they spend themselves. They refuse to quit. Possessing an enormous amount of enthusiasm for their labor, they press on regardless of the odds, virtually unconcerned with the obstacles. Actually, they are like pioneers—resilient and rugged. They're tireless.

Even if you're not starting, you have to believe that you're as good as the guy who's playing in front of you. I've been second-string three times in my football career, and each time I thought I was better than the guy in front of me.

If you let one game or one play haunt you, your mind's in the wrong place.

There are two types of preparation—physical and mental. You can't get by with just one or the other.

Excellence
Anonymous

It is achieved in an organization only as a result of an unrelenting and vigorous insistence in the highest standards of performance. It requires an unswerving expectancy of quality from the staff and volunteers.

Excellence is contagious. It infects and affects everyone in the organization. It charts the direction of a program. It establishes the criteria for planning. It provides zest and vitality to the organization. Once achieved, excellence has a talent for permeating every aspect of the life of the organization.

Excellence demands commitment and a tenacious dedication from the leadership of the organization. Once it is accepted and expected, it must be nourished and continually reviewed and renewed. It is a never-ending process of striving and searching. It requires a spirit of mission and boundless energy. It is always the result of a creatively conceived and precisely planned effort.

Excellence is an organization's lifeline. It is the most compelling answer to apathy and inertia. It energizes a stimulating, a pulsating, force. Once it becomes the expected standard of performance, it develops a fiercely driving and motivating philosophy of operation. Excellence is a state of mind put into action. It galvanizes an organization. It incentivizes. Stimulates. Inspires. When a climate of excellence exists, all things—staff work, volunteer leadership, finances, program—are success-driven.

Amos Alonzo Stagg

Born: West Orange, New Jersey
College: Yale, 1888
Coached: Springfield, Chicago, Pacific
Years: 57
Record: 314-199-35
Accomplishments:

- First man elected to the College Football Hall of Fame and the College Basketball Hall of Fame
- 7 Big 10 football championships
- 7 Big 10 basketball championships
- 6 Big 10 baseball championships
- Helped shape the game more than any other man. Introduced tackling dummies, play books, the huddle, direct snap from center, men in motion, reverses, numbers on uniforms, and the awarding of varsity letters.
- Voted National Coach of the Year at age 81

We are all manufacturers. Some make good. Others make trouble. And still others make excuses.

I hold with certainty that no painter, nor sculptor, nor any other artist does such excellent work as he who molds the minds and character of youth.

He doesn't smoke or drink. He doesn't chase skirts or swear. But Stagg has a vice worse than all those. He concedes himself all putts under six feet.

> —Bob Zuppke, Illinois football coach, in response to
> Stagg being referred to as "the perfect sportsman"

It was because of a promise I made to God… I have made the young men of America a ministry. I have tried to bring out the best in the boys that I have coached. I truly believe that many of them have become better Christians and citizens because of what they have learned on the athletic field.

> —Stagg, who worked with youth and coached well
> into his nineties, when asked why he coached

Everyday Success Pointers

Can't means won't try.
Your mind is the place where all progress begins and ends
To every difficulty, there is a solution.
To discover a weakness is the beginning of strength.
Your goal becomes your potential worth.
Whatever you focus your attention upon, you give strength to.
Nothing is impossible for a willing mind.
Genius is to take the complicated and make it simple.
We can change our lives by merely changing our attitudes.
To lose your fighting spirit is to lose all.
If you meet someone without a smile give them yours, it costs nothing but will pay
rich dividends.
Some people make things happen, some wait for things to happen. And then there
are those who say what happened!

The Team Link
Norm Parker, assistant coach at Iowa

I carry a link in my pocket,
A simple reminder to me,
That I am a *team* member,
No matter where I may be.
This little link is not magic,
Nor is it a good luck charm,
It isn't meant to protect me,
From any physical harm.
It's simply an understanding,
Between my teammates and me.
The link is there to remind me,
Of what a *team* member should be.
It links me to my team,
It links me to my school,
It is a constant reminder,
That football is no place for a fool.
So I carry this link in my pocket,
To remind me many a time,
That a man without conviction,
Isn't worth a simple dime.

Don't be afraid to fail. Experience is just mistakes you don't make anymore.

❖

You must love your boys to get the most out of them, I have worked with boys whom I haven't admired, but I have loved them just the same. Love has dominated my coaching career as I am sure it has and always will that of many other coaches and teachers.

❖

It Takes Men to Make Men
S.I. Hayakawa, U.S. Senator (California)

Never has it been so difficult for boys to grow up into men. Becoming a man is not a matter of chronology. It is a matter of proof. Throughout the history of mankind, boys have had to prove themselves men.

To become a man, it has always been necessary for boys to associate with men, as helpers on the father's farm, as apprentices to craftsmen, as squires to knights, as water boys to baseball teams. Through such association they learn the secrets of the adult culture: what rituals to observe, how to care for equipment, how to drink and curse and fight, how to earn and maintain the respect of other men in a society of men.

But today most boys are separated from the lives of men. Men leave for factory or office early in the morning, commuting many miles to work. They do not return until evening. Boys are brought up by mothers and school teachers.

Hence, boys often have no idea what their fathers do at work. They have no idea what a man does that makes him a man.

So the vast majority of boys are excluded from the world of men and denied the chance to exercise their powers, physical or intellectual. Is it any wonder that there is a youth problem?

Boys need challenges. Their whole being cries out for them. To face starvation, the possibility of death at enemy hands, the risks of failure in school or work or business, and to triumph over these dangers—these are the stuff of human growth, of maturity.

It takes men to make men. Mothers cannot do it by themselves. Nor can high schools. Nor colleges.

Gene Stallings
Alabama

Born: Paris, Texas
College: Texas A&M
Coached: Texas A&M, St. Louis and Phoenix Cardinals,
    Alabama
Years: 18
Record: 97-61-2
Accomplishments:
- 7 years at Alabama
- 1 national championship
- 1 SEC championship
- 4 SEC western titles
- 6 bowl games
- 70-16-1 at Alabama

A Coach's Prayer
Author Unknown

Build me an athlete, O Lord, who will be strong enough to know when he is weak and brave enough to face himself when he is afraid, one who will be proud and unbending in honest defeat and humble and gentle in victory.

Build me an athlete whose wishbone will not be where his backbone should be, an athlete who will know Thee and that to know himself is the foundation stone of knowledge. Lead him, I pray, not in the path of ease and comfort, but under the stress and spur of difficulties and challenge. Here let him learn to stand up in the storm; here let him learn compassion for those who fall.

Build me an athlete whose heart will be clear, whose goal will be high; an athlete who will master himself before he seeks to master other men; one who will learn to laugh, yet never forget how to weep; one who will reach into the future yet never forget the past. And after all these things are his, I pray, a sense of humor, so as never to take himself too seriously. Give him humility, so that he may always remember the simplicity of true greatness, the open mind of true wisdom, the meekness of true strength. Then, I, his coach, will dare to whisper, "I have not lived in vain."

You play 50 or 60 plays a game for the privilege of making three or four that make the difference.

Make something happen.

❖

Never confuse activity with results.

❖

I have absolutely no problem with getting ahead and staying ahead. In fact that's our strategy.

❖

Gentle Words of Encouragement (For the Coach)
Tim Murtaugh

Spend every day preparing for the next. As you reach forward with one hand, accept the advice of those who have gone before you, and in the same manner reach back with the other hand to those who follow you; for life is a fragile chain of experiences held together by love. Take pride in being a strong link in that chain.

Discipline yourself, but do not be harsh. The pleasures of life are yours to be taken. Share them with others, but always remember that you, too, have earned the right to partake.

Know those who love you; love is the finest of all gifts and is received only to be given. Embrace those who truly love you; for they are few in a lifetime…
Then return that love tenfold, radiating it from your heart to fill their lives as sunlight warms the darkest corners of the earth.

Love is a journey, not a destination; travel its path daily.
Do this and your troubles will be as fleeting as footprints in the sand.

When loneliness is your companion and all about you seem to be gone, pause and listen, for the sound of loneliness is silence, and in silence we hear best. Listen well, and your moments of silence will always be broken by the gentle words of encouragement spoken by those of us who love you.

Bart Starr
Green Bay Packers (Quarterback)

Born: Dadeville, Alabama
College: University of Alabama, 1956
Played: Green Bay Packers
Accomplishments:
- 89-29-4 as a starter
- 6 title games, 5 championships
- 2-time MVP (first 2 Super Bowls)
- 4 times in Pro Bowl
- 17-round pick by Green Bay
- 294 passes without an interception (Green Bay)
- NFL Hall of Fame, 1977

The Substitute
Unknown Coach

To fate resigned, he waits upon the bench,
and leans his chin upon his hands.
He watches every play and vaguely hears,
the cheers that thunder from the stands.
Out there his teammates execute the plays,
His sweat and toil helped them to learn,
While he, a sub, can only watch and hope,
And patiently await his turn.

The din of cheering crowds rolls o'er his head,
unknown, the service he performs.
They only see him waiting for his chance,
The chance that often never comes.
Unsung, but still alert to give his best,
Content when thousands laud his mates,
Successful teams were never built without,
the Sub, who hopes and works and waits.

You get out of life, and out of football, exactly what you put into it. When a person realizes this and acts accordingly, he is sure to succeed

I don't think it makes sense to strive for perfection. Perfection is not attainable. I believe totally in striving for excellence, and I think there is a great deal of difference between the two. Although we strive for excellence, we should set sensible goals. One of the most frustrating things in the world is to set our goals so high that we have no chance of reaching them.

To me, team success comes before personal glory. And so it should be with you. Thank God for your talents so that you will be humble in victory and gracious in defeat. Do these things… and you will not only be a better football player, but a well-rounded person who is an asset to your team, your community, your country.

❖

Are You Strong Enough to Handle Success?
Adolph Rupp, Former University of Kentucky Basketball Coach, Record-High 876 Career Victories

Unfortunately, the road to anywhere is filled with many pitfalls, and takes a man of determination and character not to fall into them. As I have said many times, whenever you get your head above the average, someone will be there to take a poke at you. That is to be expected in any phase of life. However, as I have also said many times before, if you see a man on top of a mountain, he didn't just light there! Chance are, he had to climb through many difficulties and with a great expenditure of energy in order to get there, and the same is true of a man in any profession, be he a great attorney, a great minister, a great man of medicine, or a great businessman. I am certain he worked with a definite plan and an aim and purpose in life. I have always thought that an excerpt from Parkenham Beatty's Self-Reliance contained a good philosophy for each coach:

> By your own soul learn to live,
> and if men thwart you, take no heed,
> if men hate you, have no care;
> Sing your song, dream your dream,
> hope your hope and pray your prayer.

I am sure that if a coach will follow this philosophy of life, he will be successful. To sit by and worry about criticism, which too often comes from the misinformed or from those incapable of passing judgment on an individual or a problem, is a waste of time.

Roger "The Dodger" Staubach
Dallas Cowboys (Quarterback)

Born: Cincinnati, Ohio
College: Naval Academy
Played: Dallas Cowboys
Accomplishments:
- First pro season at 27 years old
- Vietnam Veteran (Navy)
- 23 comeback victories in last two minutes of a game
- 8 playoff teams
- 4 NFC Championships
- 4 Super Bowl appearances (won 2)
- 4-time Pro Bowl player
- 1-time Super Bowl MVP
- NFC Hall of Fame, 1983

Spectacular achievements are always preceded by unspectacular preparation.

Winning isn't getting ahead of others. It's getting ahead of yourself.

When I'm in the last two minutes of a December playoff game, I'm drawing confidence from the wind sprints I did in March.

I don't aim at the bull's-eye. I aim at the center of the bull's-eye.

Hustle isn't a God-given talent like quick feet. It's something that a person develops through sheer will. It's state of mind. Every coach in the world, from the pros to the youth leagues, prays for his players to develop more hustle.

Teamwork
Author Unknown

It's all very well to have courage and skill,
And its fine to be counted a star,
But the single deed with it's touch of thrill,
Doesn't tell us the man you are.
For there's no lone hand in the game we play,
We must work to a bigger scheme,
And the thing that counts in the world today,
Is how do you pull with the team?

They may sound your praise and may call you great,
They may single you out for fame,
But you must work with your running mate,
Or never you'll win the game.
For never the work of life is done,
By the man with a selfish dream,
For the battle is lost or the battle is won,
By the spirit of the team.

You may think it's fine to be praised for skill,
But a greater thing to do,
Is to set your mind and all your will,
On the goal that's just in view.
It's helping your fellow man to score,
When his chances hopeless seem,
It's forgetting self till the game is o'er,
And fighting for the team.

Ten Characteristics of Philosopher Coaches

1. Committed to individual integrity, values, and personal growth.
2. Profound thinkers who see themselves as educators, not just coaches.
3. Well-educated (formally and informally) in a liberal arts tradition.
4. Long-run commitment to their athletes and their institution.
5. Willing to experiment with new ideas.
6. Value the coach-player relationship, winning aside.
7. Understand and appreciate human nature.
8. Love their sport and work.
9. Honest and strong in character.
10. Human and therefore imperfect.

Charles "Bud" Wilkinson
Oklahoma

Born: Minneapolis, Minnesota
College: Minnesota, 1937
Coached: Oklahoma, St. Louis Cardinals
Years: 17
Record: 145-29-4
Accomplishments:
- 47-game winning streak
- 3 national championships
- 14 Big Eight championships in 17 years
- 3 national championships as a player at Minnesota

I place him completely above words like pettiness and prejudice. Those things weren't in him.

–Prentice Gautt, the first black athlete at Oklahoma, describing Wilkinson

You can motivate players better with kind words than you can with a whip.

Every game is a chance to measure yourself against your own potential.

Once you've won or lost, it's behind you. What lies ahead is all that matters.

We are trying to build a University our football team can be proud of.

–Oklahoma school president, during Wilkinson's 47-game winning streak

Football is the American game, which embodies all of the basic principles that made America what it is. It's a game which proves that if you work a little harder, if you are willing to pay a greater physical and mental price over a longer period of time than your opponents are willing to do, you will have an excellent chance to achieve success.

More Thoughts on Football: From Players, Coaches, Writers, and Fans

If you really want to advise me, do it on Saturday afternoon between one and four o'clock, and you've got 25 seconds to do it between plays. Not on Monday. I know the right thing to do on Monday.

—Alex Agase, coach, Northwestern

❖

The harder I work, the luckier I get.

—George Allen, coach, Los Angeles Rams and Washington Redskins

❖

Losing the Super Bowl is worse than death. When you're dead you don't have to get up in the morning and read the papers.

—George Allen

❖

Any athlete with pride wants to compete against the best.

—Lance Alworth, wide receiver, San Diego Chargers

❖

When they run you out of town, make it look like you're leading a parade.

—Bill Battle, coach, Tennessee

❖

During the week I practice law. On Sunday I am the law.

—Tommy Bell, NFL official and lawyer

❖

I love the thrill of getting off a pass just before getting smashed.

—George Blanda, quarterback, Chicago Bears, Houston Oilers

You're the only person who can decide where you want to go and how you're going to get there.

–Terry Bowden, coach, Auburn (son of Bobby Bowden)

John Breen, executive, Houston Oilers, on why the Oilers' offense was ineffective: We were tipping off our plays. Whenever we broke from the huddle, three backs were laughing and one was pale as a ghost.

I think I was a Rhodes Scholar at Stanford. They asked me to hit the road both my sophomore and junior year.

–John Brodie, quarterback, Stanford, San Francisco 49ers

I feel a man has to have goals to achieve anything worthwhile. I don't think I would make 100 yards in a game very often if I didn't aim to do it.

–Jim Brown, Hall of Fame fullback, Cleveland Browns

❖

I looked at all the players in the NFL not on the Bears team as my mortal enemies. I couldn't be pals with somebody who at any moment on the field could bring an end to my utopia, playing football.

–Dick Butkus, All-American, Illinois, All-Pro, Chicago Bears

❖

I never set out to hurt anyone… Unless it was a league game or something.

–Dick Butkus

❖

Teams just beat themselves. They psyche themselves out…. They don't think they can win, so they don't. They get beat by doubt.

–Harry Carson, linebacker, New York Giants

He told me many a time, when you step on the field, it's yours. Take control. It's now your game.

—Chris Chandler, quarterback, St. Louis Rams
(married to the daughter of former 49er quarterback John Brodie)

You can accomplish almost anything as long as you don't care who gets the credit.

—Blanton Collier, coach, Cleveland Browns

Football is as American as Huckleberry Finn, apple pie, or Pluribus Unum.

—Tonto Coleman, SEC Commissioner

Al Conover, after serving as Rice football coach: I'm going to become a hog farmer. After some of the things I've been through, I regard it as a step up.

The game resembles a fast moving broadway production, with cues, settings, music, pace and hold your hats boys—A little bit of ballet.

—Bob Considine, writer, on NFL football

Running into the line, you go into a different world. All around you guys are scratching, clawing, beating on each other, feeling pain. There are noises from the crowd and from the linemen, but during that one moment, I never seem to hear them. Then, going back to the huddle, the sound of the pads slamming together will still be in my ears and I'll listen for the first time. It's too bad more people haven't been in there, where football is really played.

—Larry Csonka, Al-Pro fullback, Miami Dolphins

What it's like to catch a pass and be tackled at the same time is like being hit by a truck while walking with a bag of groceries and having the people on the sidewalk boo you for dropping the bag.

—Al Denson, receiver, Denver Broncos

These things are necessary on your squad to allow the players to feel committed to the game:
- A sincere, wholesome respect for one another.
- A feeling of sensitivity by the coaches to the academic and social problems of a student athlete.
- A sincere desire to help the student athlete.
- Fairness and honesty—the player cannot feel the reason I'm not playing is coach doesn't like me.
- Maybe the most important—there are enough people sitting around the locker room to stop the guy who is always complaining.

–Dan Devine, coach, Arizona State, Missouri, Notre Dame,
Green Bay Packers

In the football business, if you're standing still, you're losing ground.

–Doug Dickey, coach, Tennessee

The first couple of plays, I'm super aggressive. I'm out of my stance and on the guy.... I want to establish that he's going to get manhandled.

–Dan Dierdorf, All-American, Michigan, All-Pro, St. Louis Cardinals

Football is full speed. All the stops are out. Caution is to the wind, and you're battling with everything you have. That's the real fun of the game.

–Dan Dierdorf

If I can beat a guy in his mind, everything else falls into place.

–Dan Dierdorf

There are no office hours for champions.

–Paul Dietzel, coach, Miami of Ohio, Army, LSU

The athletic field is very democratic. Each person is judged by what he does rather than color, religion, nationality, hometown, or personal wealth or prestige.

—Paul Dietzel

❖

Football is as primitive as hand to hand combat. No quarter is asked or given.

—Terry Donahue, coach, UCLA

❖

Doubt is what makes you miss tackles!

—Roger "Rocky" Donnahoo, defensive back, New York Jets

❖

Art Donovan, former 310-pound Baltimore Colts defensive lineman, claiming he's a light eater: As soon as it's light, I start to eat.

❖

Win or lose, one thing is always the same—you can't relax.

—Bill Dooley, coach, Virginia Tech

❖

Borrow from other coaches. Pick and choose the things that work for you. But you've got to coach to suit your own personality.

—Bill Dooley

❖

An atheist is a guy who watches a Notre Dame—SMU football game and doesn't care who wins.

—Dwight D. Eisenhower, President of the United States

❖

Humility is always one play away.

—Tim Foley, safety, Miami Dolphins

When you lose, you doubt yourself and your plans. Losing creates doubt just like winning creates momentum.

–Danny Ford, coach, Clemson, Arkansas

I want to coach a team that opponents don't look forward to playing.

–Danny Ford

In order to win, you must expect to win. You might even call it the arrogance factor.

–Dan Fouts, quarterback, San Diego Chargers

The key is to concentrate your way through the bad times. I really believe that you can have some of your best games that way. You play better because you have to concentrate harder.

–Dan Fouts

A coach has to fit into the mode of the school, the community, and the state.

–Bob Fulton, sportscaster, South Carolina

If you play this game for money or fame it won't mean anything to you or anybody else. You have to play it for your team, yourself, and your family and the people who come to see you. It's pure passion.

–Eddie George, running back, Tennessee, Dallas Cowboys

Winning is important. Winning has a joy and discrete purity that cannot be replaced by anything else. Winning is important to everyone's sense of satisfaction and well-being. It is not everything, but it is something powerful, indeed beautiful, in itself.

–A. Bartlett Giamatti, president, Yale

A good coach needs a patient wife, a loyal dog, and a great quarterback, but not necessarily in that order.

–Bud Grant, coach, Minnesota Vikings

❖

Start from scratch and keep on scratching.

–Dennis Green, coach, Minnesota Vikings, Arizona Cardinals, Stanford, Northwestern

❖

Old place kickers never die, they just go on missing the point.

–Lou Groza, placekicker, Cleveland Browns

❖

It is one of the strange ironies of life. Those who work the hardest, who subject themselves to the strictest discipline, who give up certain pleasurable things in order to achieve a goal, seem to be the happiest people.

–Brutus Hamilton, Olympic track coach

❖

I don't talk about my battle plan after a victory. I save it for another game down the line.

–George Halas, coach, Chicago Bears

❖

Terry Hanratty, former Notre Dame quarterback, when asked whether his college uniform number had been retired: If they retired the numbers of all the greats at Notre Dame, there wouldn't be any numbers left.

❖

My priorities in life are faith, family, and football, in that order.

–Mike Holmgren, coach, Green Bay Packers (1997 Super Bowl champions), Seattle Seahawks

❖

E. J. Holub, former linebacker, Kansas City Chiefs, on his 12 knee operations: My knees look like they lost a knife fight with a midget.

Close only counts in ballroom dancing, horseshoes, and hand grenades:

—Frank Howard, coach, Clemson

❖

Everything cometh to him that waiteth, so long as he who waiteth worketh like hell while he waiteth.

—Frank Howard

❖

I bought a cemetery plot overlooking Memorial Stadium. That's where I'll spend all eternity, listening to the cheers for my Tigers.

—Frank Howard

❖

I retired for health reasons. The alumni got sick of me.

—Frank Howard

❖

Leroy Irvin, defensive back, Kansas, on why he talks to opposing receivers: I just want 'em to know who's robbin' the train.

❖

The game is the star of the show. My only job is to help the audience enjoy it.

—Keith Jackson, TV announcer

❖

To Southerners, football is as essential as air conditioning.

—Dan Jenkins, writer

❖

Kickers are like golfers: 90 percent confidence, 9 percent technique, and 1 percent ability.

—Jimmy Johnson, coach, Oklahoma State, University of Miami, Dallas Cowboys, Miami Dolphins

The fast life doesn't go well with football. This is a violent sport and you have to take care of your body to survive it.

–Deacon Jones, All-Pro defensive lineman, Los Angeles Rams

❖

Always remember that Goliath was a 40-point favorite over Little David.

–Shug Jordan, coach, Auburn

❖

I don't believe in a jinx or a hex. Winning depends on how well you block and tackle.

–Shug Jordan

❖

I grew up pickin' cotton on my daddy's farm. To me, football is like a day off.

–Lee Roy Jordan, linebacker, All-American, Alabama, All-Pro, Dallas Cowboys

❖

If you could have won, you should have won.

–Chuck Knox, Coach, Buffalo Bills, Seattle Seahawks

❖

Teamwork teaches that each member of the organization must sacrifice–for the good of everyone.

–Frank Leahy, coach, Notre Dame

❖

A football game is better than war; in football you don't send people out to kill or be killed. But it's still war.

–Marv Levy, coach, Buffalo Bills

❖

On game day, where else would you rather be than right here?

–Marv Levy

Temper is the only thing you can lose and still have.

–Eddie Lewis, cornerback, San Francisco 49ers

Playing cornerback is like being on an island; people can see you but they can't help you.

–Eddie Lewis

Tommy Lewis, player, Alabama, after jumping off the bench and tackling Rice All-American Dickie Moegle racing by the Alabama bench in the open field: I'm just too full of Alabama. I know I'll hear about this the rest of my life. But I had to do it.

One of my uncles was a classic paranoid who couldn't sit through a football game. He thought the guys in the huddle were talking about him.

–Franz Lidz, sportswriter

Big Daddy Lipscomb, NFL defensive tackle, on his tackling technique: I just wrap my arms around the whole backfield and peel 'em off one by one until I get to the ballcarrier. Him I keep.

I'm going to play every game I can, and I'm going to give it all I've got every time I play. When I get done I'm going to be able to say that I gave it hell while it lasted.

–Floyd Little, All-American, Syracuse, All-Pro, Denver Broncos

They say losing builds character. Well, I have all the character I need.

–Ray Malavasi, coach, Los Angeles Rams, after a loss

I believe football is 10% physical and 90% mental attitude. It's amazing what guys can do, or could do, if they just have the right attitude.

—Don Maynard, All-Pro, New York Jets.

❖

Set your goals up there real high, and then be serious about reaching them.

—Don Maynard

❖

If you are not practicing, just remember someone, somewhere is practicing and when you two meet, given roughly equal ability, he will win.

—Ed Macauley, basketball player, St. Louis Hawks

❖

Down in the Southeast territory, college football long ago became a geographical, historical, or social event—sometimes all three. The fans down there always have somebody they especially love to see whomped.

—John D. McCallum, sportswriter

❖

To be a great halfback, you need to be as quick as a hiccup, and you better run like you just stole a government mule.

—John Merritt, coach, Tennesse State

❖

Everyone has some fear. A man who has no fear belongs in a mental institution. Or on special teams.

—Walt Michaels, coach, New York Jets

❖

Michigan State fans, taunting Notre Dame after they went for a tie in the famous 10-10 game: Okay men, tie one for the gipper.

Southern football fans are knowledgeable, fair—and loud.

—George Mooney, writer

Bob Newhart, comedian, on his days as a high school running back: Every time I went into the line on a fake, I shouted, "I don't have it!"

After one month, each Super Bowl trophy became an antique.

—Chuck Knoll, coach, Pittsburgh Steelers (four Super Bowls)

Everyone will get beat sometime physically, but a champion seldom gets beat mentally.

—Chuck Knoll

Before you can win, you must learn not to lose it.

—Chuck Knoll

Quitting is easy, fighting is hard. Quitting is losing, fighting is winning.

—Buck Nystrom, All-American, Michigan State

If you take it easy for 10 minutes, it takes a long time to get it back, sometimes a week or two. Like everything else, concentration is a habit.

—Merlin Olsen, All-Pro, Los Angeles Rams

At the beginning of each new play, I think of it as the most important play of the year. I go into it as if the game depends on this one play.

—Merlin Olsen

Always make a total effort, even when odds are against you.

–Arnold Palmer, PGA professional

A good coach makes his players see what they can be rather than what they are.

–Ara Parseghian, coach, Notre Dame, Miami of Ohio, Northwestern

I found this sandbank by the Pearl River near my hometown, Columbia, Mississippi. I laid out a course of 65 yards or so. Sixty-five running yards on sand is like 120 on turf. But running on sand helps you make your cuts at full speed. I try to pick the heat of the day to run in, but sometimes that sand will get so hot you can't stand in one place. It'll blister your feet. You get to the point where you have to keep pushing yourself. You stop, throw up, and push yourself again. There's no one around to feel sorry for you.

–Walter Payton, running back, Chicago Bears

I want players to think as positively as the 85-year-old man who married a 25-year-old woman and bought a five-bedroom house next to the elementary school.

–Charley Pell, coach, Clemson, Florida

There are two ways to build a team. Either get better players or get the ones you got to play better.

–Bum Phillips, coach, Houston Oilers

❖

Two kinds of players ain't worth a damn. One that never does what he is told and the other that does nothing except what he's told.

–Bum Phillips

❖

There are two types of coaches. Them that just been fired and them that are going to be fired.

–Bum Phillips

I wouldn't say Earl Campbell was in a class by himself, but I can tell you one thing: It sure don't take long to call the roll.

–Bum Phillips

❖

I'd rather have a self-made player than a natural player. I'd rather have a guy with less talent who works than one with more talent who doesn't work.

–Bum Phillips

❖

The way you win is to get average players to play good and good players to play great.

–Bum Phillips

❖

Nothing is opened by mistake as often as one's mouth.

–Bum Phillips

❖

The main thing is getting people to play. When you think it's your system that's winning, you're in for a damn big surprise.

–Bum Phillips

❖

The coach is the team, and the team is the coach. You reflect each other.

–Tommy Prothro, coach, UCLA, San Diego Chargers

❖

I left because of illness and fatigue. The fans were sick and tired of me.

–John Ralston, coach, Denver Broncos, Stanford

❖

Difficulties in life are intended to make us better, not bitter.

–John Ralston

You never get comfortable in this game.
                                    –Dan Reeves, player, Dallas Cowboys

A streak of fire, a breath of flame eluding all who reach and clutch. A gray ghost sent into the game that rival hands may rarely touch. A rubber, bounding, blasting soul whose destination is the goal. Red Grange of Illinois!
                                    –Grantland Rice, sportswriter

Dave Rimington, Nebraska offensive lineman, after lifting a piano into place at a team banquet so teammates could sing and play: The coaches speak of skilled and nonskilled positions. Now I know the difference. Moving the piano is non-skill. Playing the piano is skill.

An angry football team is better than a confident one.
                                    –Pepper Rodgers, coach, Kansas, UCLA, Georgia Tech

Do the very best you can with what you have.
                                    –Theodore Roosevelt, President of the United States

He is Jack Dempsey, Babe Ruth, Al Jolson, Paavo Nurmi, and Man o' War all rolled into one.
                                    –Damon Runyon, sportswriter, on Red Grange

If you don't have the best of everything, make the best of everything you have.
                                    –Erk Russell, coach, Georgia Southern

If you're gonna be a winner, you got to have a bad case of the wants.
                                    –Erk Russell

When you finally reach the solution it is very self-supporting. It confirms in your mind that you can do it, that if you try hard and keep chipping away, you'll get there. A proper solution validates all your effort.

–Frank Ryan, quarterback, Cleveland Browns

My trick was to prepare my psychology in advance. I worked on my mind all week every week…. The goal was to have a mind completely trustworthy. It was an interesting challenge.

–Frank Ryan

I don't want our men to die for our cause. I want to make the other guys die for theirs.

–Nick Saban, coach, Michigan State, LSU

Red Sanders, upon becoming head coach at UCLA: I expected to find the Hollywood types sitting around a swimming pool with a martini in one hand and a wet blond in the other. Actually, that's an exaggeration. Some of these fellows don't like martinis.

Football is football. The best high school players usually make the best college players, and the best college players usually make the best pro players. It's just that the cream gets a little thinner as you go along.

–Kenneth Sims, defensive lineman, New England Patriots

❖

My trouble today is that I am now coaching one of the teams I'd always wanted to play.

–Steve Sloan, All-American, Alabama, coach, Vanderbilt, Texas Tech

❖

You can motivate by fear and you can motivate by reward. But both methods are only temporary. The only lasting motivation is self-motivation.

–Homer Smith, coach, Army

We finally got Nebraska where we want them – off our schedule.
                                    –Cal Stoll, coach, University of Minnesota

When I got into coaching I adopted the philosophy that yesterday is a canceled check, today is cash on the line, and tomorrow is a promissory note.
                                    –Hank Stram, coach, Kansas City Chiefs

Embarrassment is a great motivator. There are some people who play very, very well just so they don't get embarrassed in front of their friends and a national audience.
                    –Lynn Swann, All-American, Southern Cal, All-Pro, Pittsburgh Steelers

The longer I live, the more I realize the impact of attitude on life. Attitude, to me is more important than facts. It is more important than the past, than education, than money, than circumstances, than failures, than successes, than what other people think or say or do. It is more important than appearance, giftedness, or skill. It will make or break a company, a church, a home. The remarkable thing is we have a choice every day regarding the attitude we will embrace for that day. I am convinced that life is 10% what happens to me and 90% how I react to it. And so it is with you. We are in charge of our attitudes.
                                    –Charles Swindoll, minister

Leadership must be demonstrated, not announced.
                                    –Fran Tarkenton, quarterback, Minnesota Vikings

You can last a little longer if you know when to hit the big licks and when to avoid them.
                                    –Jim Taylor, All-Pro, Green Bay Packers

Lawrence Taylor, linebacker, New York Giants, after 12 seasons in the NFL: When I get out of bed in the morning it sounds like my body is making popcorn.

Playing professional football for the Canton Bulldogs was the best time of my life. I'll never forget it.

—Jim Thorpe, one of the great athletes of all time

In reading the lives of great men, I found that the first victory they won was over themselves.

—Harry S. Truman, President of the United States

It's a lot tougher to be a football coach than a president. You've got four years as a president, and they guard you. A coach doesn't have anyone to protect him when things go wrong.

—Harry S. Truman

I never did give anybody hell, I just told the truth and they thought it was hell.

—Harry S. Truman

My definition of a fan is the kind of guy who will scream at you from the 160th row of the bleachers because he thinks you missed a marginal holding call in the center of the interior line, and then after the game can't find his car in the parking

—Jim Tunney, NFL referee

You may fail a thousand times, but success may be hiding behind the next play. You never know how close victory is unless you continue full speed.

—Bob Tyler, coach, Mississippi State

There is a difference between conceit and confidence. A quarterback has to have confidence. Conceit is bragging about yourself. Confidence means that you believe you can get the job done. I have always believed that I could get the job done.

—Johnny Unitas, quarterback, Baltimore Colts

The worst thing a coach can do is stand pat and think the things that worked yesterday will win tomorrow. Intelligent changes must be made.

—Johnny Vaught, coach, Tennessee

❖

If you don't invest very much, then defeat doesn't hurt very much, and winning than really isn't very exciting.

—Dick Vermeil, coach, UCLA, St. Louis Rams, Kansas City Chiefs

❖

Good players, not big players, win games for you.

—Pappy Waldorf, coach, UCIA

❖

I never get tired of running with the ball. The ball ain't that heavy.

—Herschel Walker, All-American, University of Georgia, Dallas Cowboys, Philadelphia Eagles

❖

If skill is about the same, I'll take the all-outer over the in-and-outer every time.

—Pop Warner, coach, University of Pittsburgh

❖

If lessons are learned in defeat, our team is really getting a great education.

—Murray Warmath, coach, University of Minnesota

❖

Associate yourself with men of good quality if you esteem your own reputation, for it is better to be alone than in bad company.

—George Washington, President of the United States

❖

True grit is making a decision and standing by it, doing what must be done—for no moral man can have peace of mind if he leaves undone what he knows he should have done.

—John Wayne, actor, former player, Southern Cal

Be more concerned with your character than your reputation, because your character is what you really are; your reputation is merely what others think you are.

–John Wooden, basketball coach, UCIA

The 8 laws of learning are explanation, demonstration, imitation, repetition, repetition, repetition, repetition, and repetition.

–John Wooden

My advice for defensive players: Take the shortest route to the ball and arrive in a bad humor.

–Bowden Wyatt, coach, Tennessee

Bill Yeoman, coach, University of Houston, on one of his 300-pound linemen being declared ineligible because of poor grades: For a big man he can really move well. He just can't move to class.

It's brutal. The minute a man leaves a team he's isolated, so is his family. The other players feel, I better not let him touch me. It's just like falling off a cliff.

–Steve Young, quarterback, San Francisco 49ers

Bob Zuppke, coach, on all-time All-American Red Grange, who wore #77 at Illinois: He was such a natural I gave him #7, a natural in shooting dice. He got so much better I gave him two.

What Is a Football Player?

Charles Loftus, Director of Sports Information, Yale University

Between the innocence of boyhood and the dignity of man, we find a sturdy creature called a football player. Football players come in assorted weights, heights, jersey colors, and numbers, but all great football players have the same creed: to play every second of every minute of every period of every game to the best of their ability.

Football players are found everywhere—underneath, on top of, running around, jumping over, passing by, twisting from, or diving through the enemy. Teammates rib them, officials penalize them, students cheer them, kid brothers idolize them, coaches criticize them, college girls adore them, alumni tolerate them, and mothers worry about them. A football player is Courage in cleats. Hope in a helmet. Pride in pads, and the best of Young Manhood in moleskins.

When your team is behind, a football player is incompetent, careless, indecisive, lazy, uncoordinated, and stupid. Just when your team threatens to turn the tide of battle, he misses a block, fumbles the ball, drops a pass, jumps offside, runs the wrong way, or completely forgets his assignment.

A football player is a composite—he eats and sleeps like Notre Dame, but more often than not, plays like Grand Canyon High. To an opponent publicity man, he has the speed of a gazelle, the strength of an ox, the size of an elephant, the cunnings of a fox, the agility of an adagio dancer, the quickness of a cat, and the ability of Red Grange, Glen Davis, Bronko Nagurski, and Jim Thorpe—combined.

To his own coach he has, for press purposes, the stability of mush, the fleetness of a snail, the mentality of a mule, is held together by adhesive tape, bailing wire, sponge rubber, and has about as much of a chance of playing on Saturday as would his own grandfather.

To an alumnus a football player is someone who will never kick as well, run as far, block as viciously, tackle as hard, fight as fiercely, give as little ground, score as many points, or generate nearly the same amount of spirit as did those particular players of his own yesteryear.

A football player likes game films, trips away from home, practice sessions without pads, hot showers, long runs, whirlpool baths, recovered fumbles, points after touchdowns, long field goals, cold coke at halftime, his best girl waiting outside the locker room, his name in the paper and the quiet satisfaction that comes from being part of a perfectly executed play. He is not much for wind sprints, sitting on the bench, rainy days, ankle wraps, scouting reports, calisthenics, or coaches in his face.

No one else looks forward so much to September or so little to December. Nobody gets as much pleasure out of knocking down, hauling out, or just plain bringing down the enemy. Nobody else can cram into one mind assignments for an end-run, an off-tackle slant, a jump pass, a quarterback sneak, a drive play, punt protection, kick-off returns, screen pass, designed to result in a touchdown every time it is tried.

A football player is a wonderful creature—you can criticize him, but you can't make him quit. You can get him out of a game, but you can't get him out of football. Might as well admit it—be you alumnus, coach or fan—he is your personal representative on the field, your symbol of fair and hard play. He may not be an All-American, but he is an example of the American way. He is judged, not for his race nor for his religion, nor for his social standing, and not for his finances, but by the democratic yardstick of how well he blocks, tackles, and sacrifices individual glory for the overall success of his team.

He is a hard-working, untiring, determined kid doing the best he can for his school or college. And when you come out of a stadium, grousing and feeling upset that your team has lost, he can make you mighty ashamed with just two sincerely spoken words—"We tried!"

About the Author

Larry Bielat is an international motivational speaker. He coached football for 35 years at every level—high school, college (University of Colorado, University of New Mexico, Pittsburgh, MSU), and professional (USFL's Philadelphia Stars). The author of seven books, Bielat is a former Michigan State University quarterback, Assistant Alumni Director, and radio color analyst for MSU Spartan football.

In high school, Bielat was an All-American quarterback. He lettered three years in football at MSU and was the first quarterback of the New York Jets. He was also offered a baseball contract by the New York Yankees.

Bielat and his wife, Lois Hilden, live in Gulf Shores, Alabama. They have four children and 11 grandchildren.